The Antarctic: A Very Short Introduction

VERY SHORT INTRODUCTIONS are for anyone wanting a stimulating and accessible way into a new subject. They are written by experts, and have been translated into more than 45 different languages.

The series began in 1995, and now covers a wide variety of topics in every discipline. The VSI library now contains over 500 volumes—a Very Short Introduction to everything from Psychology and Philosophy of Science to American History and Relativity—and continues to grow in every subject area.

Titles in the series include the following:

AFRICAN HISTORY John Parker and Richard Rathbone
AGEING Nancy A. Pachana
AGNOSTICISM Robin Le Poidevin
AGRICULTURE Paul Brassley and Richard Soffe
ALEXANDER THE GREAT Hugh Bowden
ALGEBRA Peter M. Higgins
AMERICAN HISTORY Paul S. Boyer
AMERICAN IMMIGRATION David A. Gerber
AMERICAN LEGAL HISTORY G. Edward White
AMERICAN POLITICAL HISTORY Donald Critchlow
AMERICAN POLITICAL PARTIES AND ELECTIONS L. Sandy Maisel
AMERICAN POLITICS Richard M. Valelly
THE AMERICAN PRESIDENCY Charles O. Jones
AMERICAN SLAVERY Heather Andrea Williams
THE AMERICAN WEST Stephen Aron
AMERICAN WOMEN'S HISTORY Susan Ware
ANAESTHESIA Aidan O'Donnell
ANARCHISM Colin Ward
ANCIENT EGYPT Ian Shaw
ANCIENT GREECE Paul Cartledge
THE ANCIENT NEAR EAST Amanda H. Podany
ANCIENT PHILOSOPHY Julia Annas

ANCIENT WARFARE Harry Sidebottom
ANGLICANISM Mark Chapman
THE ANGLO-SAXON AGE John Blair
ANIMAL BEHAVIOUR Tristram D. Wyatt
ANIMAL RIGHTS David DeGrazia
ANXIETY Daniel Freeman and Jason Freeman
ARCHAEOLOGY Paul Bahn
ARISTOTLE Jonathan Barnes
ART HISTORY Dana Arnold
ART THEORY Cynthia Freeland
ASTROPHYSICS James Binney
ATHEISM Julian Baggini
THE ATMOSPHERE Paul I. Palmer
AUGUSTINE Henry Chadwick
THE AZTECS David Carrasco
BABYLONIA Trevor Bryce
BACTERIA Sebastian G. B. Amyes
BANKING John Goddard and John O. S. Wilson
BARTHES Jonathan Culler
BEAUTY Roger Scruton
THE BIBLE John Riches
BLACK HOLES Katherine Blundell
BLOOD Chris Cooper
THE BODY Chris Shilling
THE BOOK OF MORMON Terryl Givens
BORDERS Alexander C. Diener and Joshua Hagen
THE BRAIN Michael O'Shea
THE BRICS Andrew F. Cooper
BRITISH POLITICS Anthony Wright

Klaus Dodds

THE ANTARCTIC

A Very Short Introduction

OXFORD
UNIVERSITY PRESS

OXFORD
UNIVERSITY PRESS

Great Clarendon Street, Oxford ox2 6DP,
United Kingdom

Oxford University Press is a department of the University of Oxford.
It furthers the University's objective of excellence in research, scholarship,
and education by publishing worldwide. Oxford is a registered trade mark of
Oxford University Press in the UK and in certain other countries

British Library Cataloguing in Publication Data
Data available

Library of Congress Cataloging in Publication Data
Data available

ISBN 978-0-19-969768-7

Printed and bound by
CPI Group (UK) Ltd, Croydon, CR0 4YY

Contents

Acknowledgements

Writing a *Very Short Introduction* to Antarctica is a task not for the faint-hearted. As an object of study, it has attracted a thoroughly interdisciplinary array of scholarship. Much of this research has been scientific, within the environmental and physical sciences, addressing both Antarctica as a physical entity as well as relating it to broader debates about anthropogenic climate change. More recently, the social sciences and humanities (including the creative arts) have played their part in scrutinizing our ongoing engagement to a continent lacking indigenous human population. Like their scientific counterparts, they are also eager to research and ruminate on a place that is as much an archive (of past climate history and human encounter) as it is an opportunity to make sense of an object of anthropocentric panic. Once upon a time, the ice was to be feared; now, it is increasingly being mourned as it cracks, melts, and evaporates.

I have had to make some difficult choices along the way. It would be quite possible to write a *Very Short Introduction* to Antarctica and concentrate entirely on scientific debates, and the role of the physical sciences in helping to better understand the region's complex environment. I have also given less weight to the first-hand experiences of Antarctica, and to some of the fascinating insights that these might offer about living in an extremely cold and isolating environment. On balance, this is a *Very Short*

Introduction to the human geographies of Antarctica, with a strong emphasis on definitions, discovery, exploration, treaties, disputes, and governance.

To make those difficult choices, I have been fortunate enough to be able to turn to a number of people for guidance. My Austrian mother remains a wise *Chefredakteur*. I thank Alan Hemmings and Peder Roberts for their editorial guidance and insights. In terms of Antarctic science, I am most grateful for the advice provided by the following polar scientists: Mike Bentley, Huw Griffiths, Martin Seigert, Colin Summerhayes, and Eric Wolf – if I have made errors, then it is my fault entirely. Over the years, I have greatly valued conversations with Christy Collis, Elena Glasberg, and Adrian Howkins. My colleagues at Royal Holloway continue to contribute to a very congenial working environment, and sabbatical leave in 2010–11 is acknowledged. I thank the Master and Fellows of St Cross College, University of Oxford, for a visiting fellowship in academic year 2010–11, and the long-term support of the British Antarctic Survey and the Scott Polar Research Institute, University of Cambridge. Colleagues at Oxford University Press were a pleasure to work with, and I thank Andrea Keegan and Kerstin Demata for commissioning this *Very Short Introduction* in the first place – they also commissioned two readers' reports, which were insightful and generous in spirit. Thank you also to Kay Clement for her proof reading of the manuscript. Bradley Garrett very kindly prepared the index for this book.

For supporting my Antarctic, and increasingly Arctic, passions, I owe a debt of gratitude to my family, and in particular my wife, Carolyn. It is she who looks after our base camp in Richmond upon Thames, and tolerates my frequent absences to the polar world and beyond. But I hope she will forgive me if I dedicate this book to our two children, Alex and Millie, for our shared enjoyment of the antics of four fictional penguins – Skipper, Rico, Kowalski, and Private.

List of illustrations

Chapter 1
Defining the Antarctic

The German geophysicist Alfred Wegener (1880–1930) developed the theory of continental drift, which postulated that the Antarctic was part of an ancient super-continent called Pangaea. Created some 300 million years ago, this super-continent broke up 100 million years later to establish the current configuration of continents. Publicly articulated in 1912, the year of Captain Robert Scott and his party's demise in the Antarctic, Wegener's thesis was made possible in part by educated guesswork but also through accumulating knowledge of the continents, and their underlying geology. The Antarctic continent was the last to be discovered by humans even if its presence was postulated far earlier. In 1773/4, the British explorer Captain James Cook saw at first hand the potential for an additional landmass. Over the following hundred years, outlying islands and the coastal portion of the Antarctic was sighted, charted, and partially explored.

Ushering in a new era of continental exploration and international rivalry, the Antarctic is now as much a symbol of global anxiety (with associated rescue fantasies), as it is a site of ongoing scientific collaboration and knowledge exchange – snow, ice, and the cold are new geopolitical and scientific front lines.

Tracing the Antarctic

The Antarctic has been defined and delineated with reference to latitude, climatic characteristics, ecological qualities, political and legal boundaries, as well as through appeals to its sublime wilderness and endangerment. There is some congruence between these spatial definitions but also important gaps. Some definitions are more tightly defined while others emphasize how the Antarctic might be thought of in more elastic, even fuzzy, terms.

Defining the sub-Antarctic

This refers in the main to island groups that lie close and sometimes north of the Antarctic Convergence – where the colder waters of the Southern Ocean meet the warmer waters of the Atlantic, Pacific, and Indian Oceans. These groups include Bouvet Island, the Kerguelen Islands, and the South Sandwich Islands. Unlike the Antarctic continent, countries such as Britain, France, Australia, New Zealand, and South Africa exercise sovereignty over these islands. Thus, they are in the main subject to undisputed territorial seas, exclusive economic zones, and continental shelf rights.

However, the ownership of some sub-Antarctic islands, such as South Georgia and South Sandwich, are disputed, in this case involving a long-standing disagreement between Britain and Argentina. In April 1982, the two countries were drawn into conflict over South Georgia and, further to the north, the Falkland Islands/Islas Malvinas. There are other islands, which are not considered sub-Antarctic *sensu stricto*, for example Southern Oceanic islands such as Gough and Auckland.

The Antarctic as an area, according to geographical convention at least, refers to everything below the *Antarctic Circle*, including ice shelves and water. The Antarctic Circle is distinguished from

Antarctica, which refers to the landmass that is the southern polar continent. While the two terms are often used interchangeably, this is a fundamental distinction, as the area south of the Antarctic Circle (defined as 66°S of the Equator) experiences at least one day of continuous daylight every year (the December solstice), and a corresponding period of continuous night-time at least once per year (the June solstice). When it comes to the governance of the Antarctic, the *Antarctic Convergence* (see Figure 1) has also been used to manage activities such as fishing.

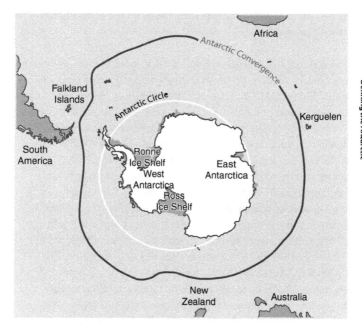

1. The Antarctic Convergence represents an important climatic boundary between air and water masses, and is also an approximate boundary for the Southern Ocean, surrounding the Antarctic continent. The water around the land mass is cold and with a slightly lower salinity than north of the convergence zone. The area is also rich in nutrients, providing a key support for the ecosystems in the Southern Ocean

Geographical latitude is only one possible register of the Antarctic. For the Swedish geologist Otto Nordenskjold, writing in 1928, the polar regions were defined by their coldness. Characterized as desert-like, with annual precipitation of only 200 millimetres along the coast and less in the interior, only specially adapted plant and animal life was thought to be able to endure. As Nordenskjold concluded, 'Nowhere on earth is nature so completely and directly characterized by the daily regular weather – by what we might call the normal climate – as in the polar lands.' Temperatures in the interior of the continent can be as low as -50 °C and, at their very worst, -89 °C, recorded at the Soviet/Russian Antarctic research station on the polar plateau called Vostok.

The Antarctic Convergence (sometimes termed the 'Antarctic polar front' or the 'polar frontal zone'), where the cold body of water that is the Southern Ocean meets the warmer waters of the Indian, Pacific, and Atlantic Oceans, provides another definition of the Antarctic. Rather than a latitudinal delineation, we have here an oceanographic/climatic frontier that acts as a zone of transition emphasizing movement and connection. The convergence itself varies from year to year, depending on sea temperature and climatic trends. So these are flows that make, remake, and unmake a zone of some 30–50 kilometres in width, encircling the polar continent, and stretching north of South Georgia and Bouvet Island. It roughly coincides with the mean February isotherm (10°C) and lies around 58°S, considerably north of the Antarctic Circle. Air and sea surface temperatures change markedly once one crosses the Antarctic Convergence. In resource management terms, the Antarctic Convergence is significant because of the wealth of marine life, especially plankton and shrimp-like krill – the food of choice of birds, fish, and whales – that is found there. As such, it also means that fishing stocks and sea birds tend to be concentrated around the Antarctic Convergence, leading to greater interest in managing these areas of the Southern Ocean.

Unlike the zonal qualities of the Antarctic Convergence, the Southern Ocean is often defined as being south of 60°S latitude, and thus encircling the continent. There is a disagreement, however. Does the Southern Ocean possess a more northerly boundary? While Captain James Cook used the term to describe the vast seas of 50°S, the International Hydrographic Organization cautiously established the boundary at 60°S in 2000. For Australians and New Zealanders, however, the water off the cities of Adelaide and Invercargill are the start of the Southern Ocean, thus consolidating their sense of these cities as 'Antarctic gateways'.

The usage of the 60°S latitude for its tentative definition of the Southern Ocean coincides with the most important political definition of the Antarctic. Article VI of the 1959 Antarctic Treaty notes:

> The provisions of the present Treaty shall apply to the area south of 60° South Latitude, including all ice shelves, but nothing in the present Treaty shall prejudice or in any way affect the rights, or the exercise of the rights, of any State under international law with regard to the high seas within that area.

This area of application entered into force in June 1961.

These lines and zones are just one way of tracing the Antarctic. In a more imaginative sense, we might acknowledge appeals to the sublime and wilderness. For 19th- and 20th-century explorers and scientists, the Antarctic was as much traced via the sublime as it was tentatively mapped and charted. As a literary expression, this notion refers to the capacity of things in nature to overwhelm the human mind by their sheer grandeur and immense possibility. A place or landscape might, as a consequence, inspire awe or provoke terror. So the sublime refers to something beyond the calculable and measurable, and more to a state of mind. The Antarctic in this particular sense is a true frontier of the human,

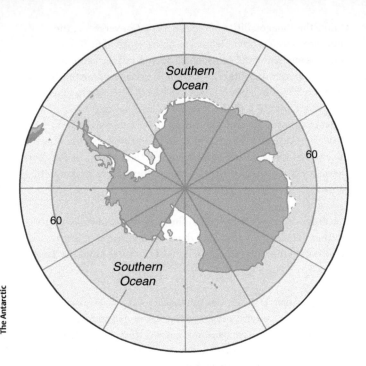

2. The Antarctic Treaty's Zone of Application

and a testing ground of men in particular. Apsley Cherry-Gerrard's memoir of Scott's last expedition, *The Worst Journey in the World* (1922), memorably referred to the Antarctic as a place of privation and suffering. As he noted caustically, 'Polar exploration is at once the cleanest and most isolated way of having a bad time which has been devised.' But it could also be compelling, as Cherry-Gerrard noted, 'And I tell you, if you have the desire for knowledge and the power to give it physical expression, go out and explore.'

The notion that the Antarctic landmass should be defined by its wilderness qualities is explicitly noted in Article 3 of the 1991

Protocol on Environmental Protection, which demands that Antarctic Treaty Consultative Parties (ATCP) commit themselves to the 'protection of the Antarctic environment... and the intrinsic value of Antarctica, including its wilderness and aesthetic values'. As well as for its own sake, Antarctica's wilderness values matter when considered as part of an ongoing global debate about the fate of the planet. Recent television programmes (e.g. the BBC's *Frozen Planet*), films (e.g. *The March of the Penguins*), music (e.g. Peter Maxwell Davies's *Antarctic Symphony*), art (e.g. Anne Noble's *British Petroleum Map*), and novels (e.g. Kim Stanley Robinson's *Antarctica*) suggest that the idea of the Antarctic landmass as wilderness provokes fascination, but also anxiety about what damage we might be doing as a human community to it. Are economic and ecological meltdown co-producing one another?

Thus, as we ponder some of the region's diverse human and physical geographies, our regional scope will extend northwards of the Antarctic Circle to encompass the northern tip of the Antarctic Peninsula, and islands such as Campbell, Prince Edward Islands, South Orkneys, and South Georgia, as well as the Southern Ocean. When we consider the Antarctic more broadly, whether it be culturally, economically, politically, or environmentally, our terms of reference will need to be ever more flexible to acknowledge bi-polar, global, and even extra-terrestrial connections, including the Moon (for parallels with Earth).

Making and unmaking the Antarctic

A satellite composite image of the Antarctic, a rather recent representation of the region, reveals a continent composed of two parts – East and West Antarctica with the western section characterized by a serpentine tail pointing towards the southern tip of the South American continent. The Southern Ocean is far removed from other continents and accompanying centres of population. The continent itself encompasses some 14,000,000 square kilometres, some 6,000,000 square kilometres larger than the United States. The coastline encompasses nearly 18,000 kilometres and is composed of a mixture of ice shelves, ice walls, rock and ice streams. The Antarctic ice sheet covers about 98% of Antarctica, and is on average 1.6 kilometres thick and some 25 million cubic kilometres in volume. The continent contains 90% of the world's ice and 70% of the world's fresh water. If the ice sheet was to melt in its entirety, then sea water levels would, it is believed, rise by some 60 metres, with devastating consequences for lower-lying regions around the world.

But this satellite image, however striking, is misleading. The Antarctic is the world's most unstable space, with extraordinary changes being recorded every year in terms of snow accumulation and sea ice extent. The satellite image literally freeze frames. Every September, in the late winter period, the size of the continent effectively doubles. A large area of the Southern Ocean extending more than 1,000 kilometres from the coastline is temporarily covered in sea ice. This capacity to alter has, over time, played havoc with attempts to map and chart the Antarctic. Countless explorers and mariners have discovered to their cost that existing maps are hopelessly inaccurate, and that there is a rich tradition of islands and coastlines being in the 'wrong place' or simply 'disappearing'.

Geologically, the Antarctic has a long and complex history, its composition ranging from Precambrian crystalline rock to glacial deposits of a recent vintage. Some of the world's oldest rock is found in the Antarctic, dating back some three billion years. Geological evidence suggests that the Antarctic has not always been characterized by the snow and cold; it was, for much of its history, a green continent. Sedimentary rocks, to be found in the Antarctic Peninsula region, reveal fossilized tropical ferns and pollen specimens, while coal deposits in the Trans-Antarctic Mountains suggests a climate favouring temperate vegetation. In the Cambrian era (590 to 505 million years ago), what we now term Antarctica was part of Gondwanaland, a super-continent composed of present-day South America, Africa, and Australia as well as parts of India, Madagascar, and New Zealand. It straddled the Equator, and layers of limestone, sandstone, and shale were deposited in tropical seas. The eastern portion of Antarctica reveals fossil evidence of marine plants such as tropical sponges. During the late Cambrian and Devonian periods (480 to 360 million years ago), the super-continent migrated towards the southern hemisphere, and some of Antarctica's oldest fossil plants found in the Trans-Antarctic Mountains have been dated to about 360 million years ago. In other areas of the polar continent such as Victoria Land, the fossilized remains of marine life have been found.

As the super-continent experienced further cooling, so glacial deposits formed, and by about 280 million years ago, Gondwanaland was located around the current location of the polar continent. But the super-continent did not remain in a fixed position, and as it moved again slightly northwards, so new flora and fauna emerged including fern-like plants, later to contribute to the formation of coal deposits in the Trans-Antarctic Mountains. The shifting environments of the Antarctic encouraged a further profusion of flora and fauna. Fossil evidence reveals the presence of not just fern plants but sea urchins, conifers, ammonites, fish fragments, and beeches. It is not hard to imagine why environmental scientists believe the Antarctic to be an extraordinarily rich archive of past climates.

Some 90–85 million years ago, in the Cretaceous period, this rich and biologically diverse super-continent began to disintegrate and transformed the southern latitudes. As Gondwanaland fragmented still further, the Atlantic, Indian, and Pacific Oceans were established, and Australia alongside Antarctica migrated southwards. Some 30–40 million years ago, Antarctica slipped even further south. This drift helped to cause the separation between the South American Andes and the Antarctic Peninsula, and in the process this tectonic schism created an oceanic passage

9

later to be named the Drake's Passage. It is only through major scientific investment, and the development of new techniques involving geophysical and remote-sensing research, that we have a better idea of the underlying geology of the polar continent and Southern Ocean. The exact mechanisms of plate movement, however, remain opaque.

The Antarctic continent possesses a series of important geological and morphological characteristics. It is a continent surrounded by a ring of water – the Southern Ocean. Due to the circumpolar current, waters circulate around the continent in a predominantly clockwise direction. There is a series of mountainous ranges, including those found on the Peninsula region, which are connected geologically to the South American Andes. Centrally, the Trans-Antarctic Mountains weave through the centre of the continent from the Weddell Sea to the north to the Ross Sea in the south. Divided into two distinct parts by the Trans-Antarctic Mountains, the East and West portions of the continent were named for their relative positions to the Greenwich meridian.

The immense Antarctic ice sheet, created over millions of years, without melting, covers the polar continent. Due to pressure brought on by the sheer weight of 13 million square kilometres of extent, the ice flows from the continental interior towards the coastline. Large slabs break off, dramatically initiating icebergs to drift outwards towards the Southern Ocean. In 2002, the Larsen B Ice Shelf splintered and was widely judged to be indicative of a warming planet. In 2008, a huge chunk of the Wilkins Ice Shelf became detached, and 570 square kilometres of ice floated out to sea. Unsurprisingly, there is much interest amongst the scientific community as to how the mass of this ice sheet has altered, and the overall ratio between accumulation and loss of ice. The changing state of the ice sheet and specific ice shelves such as the Larsen B is providing invaluable evidence of past climates, and a sobering warning of what further warming might do to other ice shelves.

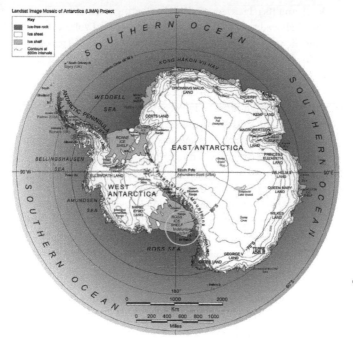

3. Ice thickness map of the Antarctic

West Antarctica is composed of the Antarctica Peninsula, Ellsworth Land, Marie Byrd Land, and the islands located within the Scotia Sea. Geologically, West Antarctica, especially the Antarctic Peninsula, is connected with a circum-Pacific chain of mountains. The Andes and the Antarctic Peninsula are, quite literally, connected to one another. The average elevation is 2,000 metres, and the chain is home to the continent's highest mountain, Mount Vinson, at 4,897 metres.

Notwithstanding these heights, a large part of West Antarctica is covered by the West Antarctic Ice Sheet (WAIS). This is a marine-based ice sheet because its base actually lies below the

11

sea level, and its edges transform into floating ice shelves. The WAIS is believed to contain about 10% of the total volume of the Antarctic ice sheet, and some two million cubic kilometres of ice press down on the underlying bedrock. While the net result has been to depress the baseline, the ice can flow at different rates over the bedrock depending on local topographies. This subterranean variability is of interest to scientists because of concerns that the WAIS may not be stable. If the WAIS disintegrates, then global sea levels could rise some 3–4 metres. In 2006, the British Antarctic Survey (BAS) warned about the possible collapse of this ice sheet, and noted that there was a danger that a tipping point might be reached thereafter accelerating ice sheet degeneration. Evidence for this change comes from research into a number of glaciers within the WAIS, coupled with observations about ocean circulation patterns around Western Antarctica that have reported a rise in ice mass loss in the period between 1996 and 2006.

East Antarctica lies on the other side of the 3,500-kilometre-long Trans-Antarctic Mountains, closer to the Indian Ocean. Geologically, the eastern portion is a stable ancient shield of Precambrian rock, similar in nature to that found in South America, South Africa, India, and Australia. It is here that the oldest rocks in Antarctica have been found, some dated to 3,900 million years ago. East Antarctica is covered by the East Antarctic Ice Sheet (EAIS), and rests on a large landmass, unlike the marine-based WAIS. It is a thicker and larger ice sheet, with a thickness of up to 4,800 metres. The South Pole is to be found on the EAIS, and beneath it lie spectacular sub-glacial lakes such as Vostok – about the size of Lake Ontario, stretching some 50 kilometres in length, and possibly created some two to three million years ago. East Antarctica is the largest and coolest portion of the polar continent, stretching from Queen Maud Land and encompassing the vast polar plateau including Wilkes Land and Victoria Land. The future stability of this part of the continent depends *inter alia* on ozone concentration coupled with weather patterns, including the polar vortex which helps to trap cold air near the South Pole.

The Antarctic coastline is immensely varied, rising steeply in places such as the mountainous Antarctic Peninsula and areas adjacent to the Ross Sea. Immense ice cliffs are to be found along much of the East Antarctic coastline. In other regions, floating ice shelves such as the Brunt Ice Shelf and the Ronne Ice Shelf represent the end point of glaciers flowing out towards the sea. Beyond the Antarctic coastline, the continental shelf falls sharply into tectonically active ocean basins, which lie anywhere between 3,000 to 6,000 metres depth. Volcanoes are to be found onshore and offshore, even if most are concentrated in western Antarctica.

Scientific curiosity remains piqued, as less than 1% of Antarctica's rock is actually accessible for direct examination, and researching the deep geology of the Southern Ocean presents considerable challenges. There is still a great deal to discover.

Life in the Antarctic

With no indigenous human population, Antarctica is unique. But we should not assume this was always well understood. One insightful vignette comes from Otto Nordenskjold's Swedish expedition (1901–4), when the soot-covered men from a lost party were at first thought to be Antarctic natives until their colleagues recognized them. The idea that soot-covered men were judged to be indigenous is telling, but perhaps they had read fictional novels such as Edgar Allan Poe's *The Narrative of Arthur Gordon Pym of Nantucket*. Poe speculates about the existence of black natives residing at the South Pole, and they eventually slaughter all but two of the American expedition who encountered them. Poe was not the only one to speculate that there might be secret and long-lost civilizations residing in the Antarctic awaiting discovery and encounter. Subterranean fiction, more generally, proved adept at representing the polar regions as entry points into a hollow Earth brimming with settlement possibilities.

In reality, the first semi-permanent human inhabitants were British and American sealers who lived on South Georgia from the late 18th century onwards. For the next 200 years, whalers and sealers, many of them Norwegian, made their home there, and hunted in the waters of the South West Atlantic. Today, governments maintain research stations, and historic huts and stores offer reminders of past and present encounters. The number of people residing on the polar continent and outlying islands varies with the summer and winter seasons. During the summer season (October–March), the numbers of scientists, and support and logistical staff, increase, up to 5,000. In the winter months, this number decreases to around 1,000 as most depart before the onset of the winter weather. The first 'indigenous' child born south of the 60° parallel was an Argentine boy called Emilio Marcos Palma, in 1978, at a research station located on the tip of the Antarctic Peninsula. His parents, along with some other families, had been sent by the Argentine government, to cement the Argentine claim to this particular part of the Antarctic. Since that period, more than ten children have been born in Antarctica in the Argentine and Chilean bases of Esperanza and Frei Montalva respectively.

Apart from the scientific community (and the military and naval personnel either living on bases and patrolling on ships) who enjoy a semi-permanent status in the Antarctic, the main inhabitants are marine and terrestrial life. Given the relatively recent isolation from other continents, and with less than 1% of land surface free of permanent snow and ice, plant communities are limited in number and scope compared to, say, a hundred million years ago. Freezing temperatures, modest soil quality, low rainfall, and a general lack of sunlight for six or more months do not represent ideal growing conditions. But plant and microbe species exist, nonetheless. It is estimated that there are something like 200 species of lichen, over 100 species of mosses and liverworts, 30 species of macro-fungi, and a profusion of algae. The short summer season is key, and even flowering plants are to be found in the milder Antarctic Peninsula. There is much research on the manner in which these species became established and indeed survived the harsh and isolated conditions in and around the polar continent. Given the limited opportunities for photosynthesis and access to water, some plant life may be hundreds, if not thousands, of years old, with very slow rates of growth and reproduction.

One of the most remarkable environments within the Antarctic where evidence of life has been found is the so-called Dry Valleys, which are located on the border between East and West Antarctica. The three valleys, named Victoria, Wright, and Taylor, encompass some 3,000 square kilometres and are unique in the sense that there is no ice or water to be found. It was once thought that rain had not fallen for at least two million years, but scientists recorded some precipitation in 1959, 1968, 1970, and 1974. The Dry Valleys were created when the terrain was uplifted in a manner whereby it actually exceeded the capacity of glaciers to cut a path through, and eventually the glaciers simply receded. When Robert Scott and his party first encountered them, they observed, 'It is certainly a valley of the dead; even the great glacier which once pushed through it has withered away.' Latter-day scientists discovered that Scott and his party were a touch premature, even though it must have been easy to imagine that nothing would survive this vast, arid, desolate place. In the 1970s, algae, bacteria, and fungi were found to be living inside the rocks scattered around the Dry Valleys. Some of these plants may date from around 200,000 years ago and survive because the rock protects the organisms from drying while at the same time enabling some moisture and light to permeate the rocks. Evidence of life has also been discovered in some of the lakes situated within the Dry Valleys, including Lake Hoare, where algae is to be found on the bottom of the lake itself. One major concern for those who study

4. The scenic view above Lake Bonney in the Dry Valleys, Antarctica

the microbes of the Dry Valleys is human disturbance, as the fragile rock and soil ecosystems are extremely vulnerable, and further change may occur if alien species and soils introduced from other continents enter the Antarctic and cross-contaminate.

Sub-glacial lakes represent another extraordinary environment within the Antarctic that might contain evidence of life. These lakes are located underneath large ice sheets. Over 150 have been identified by scientists and owe their origin to localized melting, pressure points, and geothermal heating from the earth. While ongoing research does not expect to uncover evidence of larger creatures, there may well be microbes within these sub-glacial lakes that endure an environment in which there is no light, extraordinary pressures due to the weight of the ice sheet, and temperatures that are always below zero. Sediments on the bottom of the lake might provide a food resource for such microbes. Studying these environments is an immense challenge, especially as scientists are eager to avoid any cross-contamination.

When considering the water and aerial environments, the presence of birds, seals, penguins, whales, fish, and smaller creatures such as krill is noteworthy. The Southern Ocean is immensely rich in micro-organisms such as algae and plankton and contains the coldest and densest water in the world. Consequently, more oxygen is dissolved in the sea and currents help to bring nutrients from the seabed to the surface. The surface-level algae provide food for shrimp-like krill, which in turn provide nourishment for fish, seals, whales, and birds. A marine food chain enables a reproductive cycle maintained by interdependent species. The marine ecosystem in the waters surrounding the Antarctic is comparatively simple but at the same time varied, given the life forms also found on the bottom of the ocean and sea floor such as sponges, star fish, and the like.

The bird life found in the Antarctic includes penguins and albatrosses. The penguin family includes the Adélie, Chinstrap, King, Emperor, Gentoo, Macaroni, Rockhopper, and Royal Penguin. Thanks to films such as *The March of the Penguins* and *Happy Feet*, many readers will be familiar with the Emperor Penguin, which is the largest member of the penguin family and the only one to breed on the Antarctic continent during the winter season. An adult Emperor can stand over 1 metre tall and weigh 40 kilograms and towers above the diminutive Rockhopper. Other birds include petrels, terns, skuas, and the famous albatross family, including the Amsterdam, Black-Browed, Grey-Headed, Royal, and Shy and Wandering varieties. The Wandering Albatross, associated with the poet Samuel Taylor Coleridge, is the bird of the Southern Ocean. It is truly majestic to watch as its 3.5-metre wingspan allows it to gracefully float above the sea. It is estimated that there may be around 20,000 breeding pairs scattered around the islands of the Southern Ocean such as South Georgia. However, concern has been expressed that fishing activities are having a deleterious effect on the albatross due to so-called longline fishing, whereby the birds are caught up in fishing lines and subsequently drown. Like the penguin family, krill and fish are vital elements in the diets of albatross. Some albatross can remain at sea for years, and thus never land until breeding.

Seals are a major element in the Southern Ocean and, despite being subject to intense rounds of resource exploitation alongside whales, are to be found in sizeable numbers. The species include the Fur, Crabeater, Leopard, Ross, Southern Elephant, and Weddell. While they vary in size and breeding characteristics, the Leopard Seal enjoys a formidable reputation. Adults can be over 3 metres long and weigh some 400–500 kilograms. They are largely solitary creatures, living as they do around the pack ice in the summer and sub-Antarctic islands in the winter. They eat penguins as well as other seals' pups and also fish. Some 200,000 Leopard Seals are believed to exist within the Antarctic. Under the Convention on the Conservation of Antarctic Seals (CCAS), formerly hunted seals such as the Ross and Fur varieties are now afforded protection.

Whales make the Southern Ocean a seasonal home, and were hunted in great numbers, especially in the first part of the 20th century. The Blue, Fin, Humpback, Killer, Minke, Sei, Southern Right, and Sperm varieties feed and breed in and around the Antarctic. The summer population of the Orca (Killer Whale) may exceed 80,000, and this distinctive creature with its black and white markings and tall dorsal fin was last commercially harvested in 1979–80. Other whales such as the Humpback, Blue, and Southern Right were also targeted for exploitation. The Southern Right, a slow-moving and inshore visiting species, was 'right' because it was relatively easy to kill and helpfully remained afloat once slaughtered. Oil could then be exploited in sizeable quantities, especially given that an adult Southern Right could exceed 17 metres and weigh in the region of 80–90 tons. In the mid-19th century, whalers targeted this whale and continued to do so for another hundred years. The politics of whaling is controversial as rival states continue to argue over conservation and scientific research measures.

The Southern Ocean contains more than 250 species of fish. These include some fish such as the Antarctic Ice Fish that possess an ability to survive sub-zero temperatures by producing anti-freeze glycopeptides in their blood. Other fish such as the Patagonian Toothfish have grabbed the headlines in recent years due to their intense commercial exploitation. This fish is found in cold temperate waters of the Southern Ocean, especially on seamounts and continental shelves around the sub-Antarctic islands such as Prince Edward and South Georgia. Patagonian Toothfish are slow-growing, but an adult can weigh about 10 kilograms, and mature varieties might exceed 100 kilograms. They can survive for up to 50 years and have been sold worldwide under a variety of labels such as the Chilean Sea Bass and Mero. Toothfish feed on krill, squid, and smaller fish.

Finally, we must recognize the humble 5–6-centimetre-long krill, a shrimp-like marine crustacean. Krill feed on phytoplankton and zooplankton, and their collective estimated biomass is thought to be around 500,000,000 tons. Krill is food for whales, seals, penguins, squid, and fish, as it migrates up and down the water column. Commercially, krill harvesting is carried out in the Southern Ocean, and something like 150,000 to 200,000 tons is harvested annually, mainly around the Scotia Sea. Krill is used in aquaculture, pharmaceuticals, and in sport fishing as bait. Japanese and Russian consumers also eat krill, but the volume consumed has declined since the 1980s and 1990s. At their peak, something in the order of 400,000 tons of krill was harvested in the summer season. Conservation measures were put in place in the early 1990s in order to stabilize the total catch after fears were expressed that this was another living resource being over-exploited by fishing vessels registered to the former Soviet Union and Japan. The latter remains the most important exponent of krill harvesting both in the Southern Ocean and the waters around Japan.

The geological and biological characteristics of the Antarctic are important to grasp. Antarctica's historical evolution is one fundamentally shaped by mobility not rootedness. Rather than being remote and isolated, scientists have over the last hundred years demonstrated that the Antarctic is intimately connected to a series of physical systems including the atmosphere, geology, sea level, and the evolution of planet Earth and the solar system. One example that relates well this sense of inter-connectivity is the discovery of meteorites in the Antarctic. The first meteorites were discovered in 1912, and since then more have been discovered in a variety of locations. Some 25,000 discovered specimens are helping us to better understand the creation and evolution of the solar system. The Allan Hills region is particularly fecund because it is an area in which old ice is to be found, held back by the mountains and kept snow-free by constant winds. These areas, in other words, gradually end up revealing their meteorite hoards. Many others simply drift out towards the Southern Ocean as ice sheets calve into icebergs.

The Antarctic meteorites are well preserved, and this collection of samples has been used by scientists to consider how bits of the Moon, and even Mars, may have ended up in Antarctica, after asteroids and comets impacted on those celestial bodies. One of the most famous is the ALH84001 meteorite, a Martian rock, which has been linked by American scientists to possible evidence of ancient biological activity. Scientists attached to the Antarctic Search for Meteorites (ANSMET) programme demonstrated that the Antarctic provides a rich source for experimenting and contemplating the four-billion-year-old solar system and the evolution of the planetary system. As John Carpenter's fictional film *The Thing* (1982) postulated, extra-terrestrial life might have visited the Antarctic before us. Other writers and artists, including H. P. Lovecraft in his novella *At the Mountains of Madness* (1936), speculated on the existence of past civilizations and ancient life forms once residing in the Antarctic. The figure of the scientist, such as the fictional geologist William Dyer, is critical to making sense of evidence of past life.

The Antarctic is *not* the Arctic

The Antarctic is not the Arctic. The two polar regions are distinct, and are connected with one another only in certain ways such as the migratory patterns of wildlife and, in the case of the United Kingdom, a tendency to study 'cold places' comparatively. The creation of the Scott Polar Research Institute at the University of Cambridge in the 1920s is a case in point. In other parts of the world – Canada, for example – the idea that one would study the inhabited Arctic together with a region without an indigenous human population would be treated with scepticism, and perhaps even hostility.

In a literal sense, however, 'the Antarctic' owes its origins to the Greek word for the Arctic. The Ancient Greeks named the North Pole *Arktos* (the bear), and the region lying opposite was termed as the 'Anti-Arctic', or as we know it, the Antarctic. So, at least one further way to define the Antarctic is to invoke its geographical and literal opposite. Fundamentally, the Antarctic and the Arctic are very different kinds of spaces and places. The Antarctic consists of a pole-centred continent that is mountainous and ice-covered. An ocean surrounds it. The Arctic is a polar ocean basin, which is surrounded by land, including the Euro-Asian and North American continents. The Arctic is considerably warmer than the Antarctic because so much more of the region is at sea level rather than several kilometres above it.

Biologically, too, the Antarctic is quite different to the Arctic. Whereas four million people live in the Arctic region, there is no indigenous human population in the Antarctic. Flora and fauna generally are more isolated, and there is less evidence of trans-polar migration, at least of land-based organisms, though animals such as penguins, whales, and albatrosses do migrate over sizeable distances, even connecting the Arctic and Antarctic in terms of their migratory patterns.

Economically and politically, the two polar regions are very different. The Arctic region is heavily exploited in terms of hydrocarbon commoditization alongside other forms of resource development, while the Antarctic is more limited to the realms of fishing and tourism. There is no timber sector in the Antarctic, for example. Politically, the Antarctic is governed by a treaty-based system, which prohibits all forms of mining, encourages science, and ensures that the region is demilitarized. The Protocol on Environmental Protection bans all forms of mining, even if quantities of coal, iron ore, copper, chromium, and uranium have been discovered. No one owns the Antarctic, and the international community does not recognize the seven claimant states (Argentina, Australia, Chile, France, New Zealand, Norway, and the United Kingdom). The Arctic, by way of contrast, continues to be militarized and governed by Arctic states such as Canada and Russia.

Summary

This overview is intended to provide a sense of how rich and varied our investigation of the Antarctic will need to be. The polar continent and surrounding ocean enjoy a complex geological and geographical history. The flora and fauna within the region are, in many cases, remarkably well adapted to an environment lacking in sunlight and precipitation. Yet, as we have noted, there is also plenty of evidence that Antarctica is intimately tied to other places and environments. Migratory whales and birds remind us that there are bi-polar and trans-continental considerations to bear in mind when we attempt to define the Antarctic. Globally speaking, penguins are evocative symbols of anthropogenic climate change, as with polar bears in the northern latitudes. Counter-intuitively, these two cold places are emblematic of global warming and, far from being remote, are readily imagined as indicative of global geopolitical futures.

Chapter 2
Discovering the Antarctic

Acts of discovery are never politically innocent. Even in the uninhabited Antarctic, Argentina, Britain, Russia, and the United States continue to stake their claims as discoverers. The UK-based Antarctic Place Names Committee reminds interested parties that, 'The naming of places in the Antarctic and sub-Antarctic goes back to 1775 when Capt. James Cook, RN, discovered South Georgia and the South Sandwich Islands.' So Britain, it is expected, should be considered *primus inter pares* when it comes to the discovery of the Antarctic.

States press their interests by publicizing discovery 'firsts', preserving historical huts, mobilizing memories of past explorers and their deeds, promoting contemporary tourism, and maintaining memorials (such as Lenin's bust at the Russian-based Pole of Inaccessibility research station, and the Richard Byrd bust at the American McMurdo station). Antarctic discovery and exploration are profoundly gendered, racialized, nationalized, and civilized. European and North American white men are lionized while women perform a distinctly subservient service through place names and/or providing 'Antarctic babies' for particular nationalist regimes. Non-white men are written out of the script. How many people know, for example, that the Maori Te Atu (who changed his name to John Sacs) travelled with the US Exploring Expedition in the early 1840s? For centuries, moreover, Maori believed that a white land lay to the south of contemporary New Zealand.

Initial European exploration and discovery

In the 16th and 17th centuries, European explorers and geographers were ruminating over the possible existence of a *Terra Australis*, a concept postulated as necessary since classical antiquity. European voyages around Africa demonstrated that this southerly territory was not attached to the African continent. Likewise, the voyages of Ferdinand Magellan in the 1520s, Sir Francis Drake, and the Dutch explorers Jacob Le Maire and Willem Schouten in the second half of the 16th century proved that it was not connected to the southern tip of South America. If there was another continent to be discovered, then it must reside somewhere in the poorly mapped Southern Ocean.

Although the English merchant Antonio de la Roche first discovered the island of South Georgia in 1675, the first landing was not actually made until 1775, when Captain James Cook claimed the territory for Great Britain, and named it after King George III. Cook's voyages on board *HMS Adventure* and *HMS Resolution* aimed to survey and investigate the Southern Ocean. During the second voyage of 1773, Captain Cook and his crew crossed the Antarctic Circle and came within only 70 nautical miles of the Antarctic coastline, but were forced to turn around when confronted with unrelenting sea ice.

Cook's Second Expedition of 1772–5 was instrumental in accelerating exploration, and his report published in 1777, *A Voyage towards the South Pole*, revealed his geographical ambition. Venturing into the ice-filled Southern Ocean was not for the faint-hearted:

> Thick fogs. Snow storms. Intense cold and every other thing that can render navigation dangerous, one has to encounter and these

difficulties are greatly heightened by the inexpressible horrid aspect of the country, a country doomed by nature never once to feel the warmth of the sunrays, but to lie for ever buried under everlasting snow and ice.

However, his observations about an abundant number of seals and whales played their part, perhaps unintentionally, in representing the Antarctic not as 'doomed nature' but as 'plentiful nature'. This was to prove significant in triggering further discovery and exploitation of the Antarctic, and highlighted the importance of explorers, scientists, and sailors in bringing back their stories and images of this remote land to domestic audiences.

Antarctic sightings

The first generally recognized sighting of Antarctic land occurred in the 1820s. Three individuals and their ships have been credited with this particular geographical 'first', although the islands of South Shetland and the Antarctic Peninsula are likely to have been discovered earlier by anonymous sealers. During the boom years of seal hunting, geographical knowledge was commercially sensitive and not for free exchange. It is widely accepted that the actual accolade belongs to the Estonian-born Fabian von Bellingshausen, who reported land on 27 January 1820. His expedition, involving the ships *Vostok* and *Mirnyy*, circumnavigated the polar continent, and charted the ice shelf in the northerly portion of the Antarctic Peninsula. The Irish-born Edward Bransfield's sighting, on 30 January 1820, of what was termed 'Trinity Peninsula' encouraged further reported sightings by sealers, including one Nathaniel Palmer and on his voyage in and around November 1820. It is sometimes claimed that another American sealer, John Davis, was the first to land on the polar continent in February 1821, but this is a matter of dispute amongst polar historians. The competing claims to priority have long been resources for nationalists, and continue to inform positions of the United Kingdom, United States, and Russia in relation to territorial sovereignty in the Antarctic to this day.

Sailors, scientists, and sealers contributed to the exploration and early mapping of the Antarctic Peninsula and outlying islands, many given names – like the South Shetlands and South Orkneys – that evoked the land of their discoverers. The South Shetland Islands, again claimed on behalf of the British crown, were roughly charted. Invoking King George IV, Edward Bransfield took possession of the northern tip of the Antarctic Peninsula, which was named Graham Land after the then First Lord of the Admiralty, James Graham. This was followed up by later exploratory voyages and what we might term 'claimant labour' by Henry Foster, John Biscoe, and in the 1840s, by James Clark Ross. The first three to four decades of the 19th century established a pattern of engagement with the Antarctic which proved remarkably persistent. Resources, research, and recognition proved durable bedfellows.

The United States was a noteworthy player from the start of the 19th century, and the US Congress sanctioned a major initiative to improve commercial and scientific understanding of the Pacific Ocean, but also the southerly portions of the world's major oceans. The United States Exploring Expedition (USEE) (1839–42), organized by the US Navy, sailed from Australia to explore further the possible existence of a polar continent. Traversing the Antarctic Ocean, rather than the Southern Ocean as we now describe it, the expedition gave its name to Wilkes Land – a substantial chunk of what is now called East Antarctica. Charles Wilkes was one of the explorers connected to the USEE and later had the dubious honour of being charged with 'immoral mapping' in September 1842. The charge related to his involvement in the expedition, and his claim that he had sighted a 'vast Antarctic continent', protected reportedly by an 'impenetrable barrier of ice'. Having sighted, mapped, and named it 'Wilkes Land', he was later to be accused by the British explorer Sir James Clark Ross of cartographical deceit. Wilkes, it is believed, may have unintentionally been tricked by a cloud mass, which to all appearances looked like a landmass. Whatever his cartographic merits, Wilkes's naming of a portion of the polar continent remains his legacy on the Antarctic map, as do the nineteen published volumes of the expedition that contributed to the collection of objects and ideas by the newly established Smithsonian Institution in Washington, DC (1846).

The last blank spot on the map

The period between the 1840s and 1890s represents a hiatus in the exploration and discovery of Antarctica. Whalers and sealers continued to journey to the Southern Ocean, and landings and charting were carried out across the sub-Antarctic, including the Prince Edward Islands and Heard and Macquarie Islands in the southern Indian Ocean. With seals being depleted, the rationale for further investment was less clear-cut, and public attention in Europe and North America in particular was turning northwards towards the Arctic. This was only to change in the 1890s when fresh appeals were made for a new round of exploration. The 1895 International Geographical Congress in London was a pivotal event, as geographers and cartographers appealed for fresh information about one of the world's remaining blank spaces. It was 'the greatest piece of geographical exploration still to be undertaken'. John Murray, the noted cartographer, put the appeal in the following terms in 1899:

> I always feel a little bit of shame that civilized man, living on his little planet – a very small globe – should, in this nineteenth century of the Christian era, not yet have fully explored the whole of this little area; it seems a reproach upon the enterprise, civilization, and condition of knowledge of the human race.

The resource value of the Antarctic also played a part in stimulating this swelling of interest in what Joseph Conrad

termed a more 'militant geography'. Over-exploitation of Fur
Seals, which led to the 1893 Bering Sea arbitration and the decline
of the Greenland whale fishery, focused attention on the Antarctic.
At the moment when Frederick Jackson Turner was appealing for
Americans to 'close' the American frontier, a coterie of explorers
and exploiters descended on the Antarctic. Seven major
expeditions were organized within the period between 1898 and
the 1910s involving a multi-national cast of characters and
sponsors. These included: the Belgian Antarctic Expedition
(1897–9), the British Antarctic Expedition (1898–1900), the
German Antarctic Expedition (1901–3), the first expedition by
Captain Robert Scott (the British National Antarctic Expedition,
1901–4), the Swedish Polar Expedition (1901–4), and the Scottish
National Antarctic Expedition (1902–4) led by William S. Bruce.
The net result of this extraordinary burst of endeavour was to
ensure that European and North American men were exploring
ever-greater expanses of the polar continent and surrounding
seas, and that Antarctica would become integrated in the Western
imperial economic system through whaling and meteorological
observations, to give just two of the most prominent examples.

Both public and private funding played critical roles in the
so-called 'Heroic Age' (1898–1916) of Antarctic exploration. Some
of the most notable explorers, such as the Anglo-Irish explorer Sir
Ernest Shackleton, were privately funded (even if his initial
experience came from being a participant of the Discovery
Expedition in 1901–4). Sent home early from the Discovery
Expedition due to ill health, Shackleton led the Nimrod
Expedition (1907–9), funded by the Scottish industrialist Sir
William Beardmore, and in January 1909, he and his three
companions trekked across the polar continent and reached the
furthest southerly point thus far achieved. At latitude 88°S, they
were approximately 110 miles from the South Pole (the publicly
disseminated figure of 97 miles was judged to have more of a
dramatic ring to it). They also made the first ascent of Mount
Erebus and claimed to have reached the South Magnetic Pole,

though later evaluation showed the three-man party's calculations were probably in error. King Edward VII knighted Shackleton for that extraordinary achievement, appropriately termed by fellow expedition member Frank Wild as 'the great southern journey'. Famously, the decision to turn back from their final destination, the South Pole, was immortalized in the expedition account, *The Heart of the Antarctic*, as a decision based on a judgement that it was better to be 'a live donkey than a dead lion'. These words were to acquire a prophetic quality.

The cumulative impact of this exploratory endeavour was mixed. On the one hand, these overwhelmingly European expeditions sponsored by a combination of industrialists, commercial companies, government departments, and academic societies led to ever greater areas of the Antarctic being visited, explored, and studied. On the other hand, the reported discoveries were of variable quality, with complaints that maps and charts were incomplete and irreconcilable. The physical geography of the Antarctic remained confusing and confused. As a consequence, there appeared to be plenty of new geographical milestones to strive for, none greater than the geographic pole.

Racing to the pole

Coinciding with the invention of the modern Olympics, the 'race to the pole' was driven by a combination of geopolitical, imaginative, and scientific ambition. Shackleton's Nimrod Expedition (1907–9) played a notable role in alerting others to the glaciated geography of the interior. As Edward Larson notes in his book *An Empire of Ice*, men like Robert Scott, Ernest Shackleton, and the Anglo-Australian Douglas Mawson were agents of the British Empire but they were also curious about the environments they encountered. This was also the case for other Europeans such as the Norwegian Roald Amundsen and the German explorer/scientist Wilhelm Filchner. Amundsen's Fram/South Pole Expedition (1910–12), involving four sledges, up to 52 dogs, and five men, arrived at the South Pole on 14 December 1911, and named the Antarctic Plateau, King Haakon VII Plateau. About the same time, the Japanese Antarctic Expedition (1910–12) led by Nobu Shirase encountered Amundsen's ship the *Fram*, which was moored in the Bay of Whales. The Japanese party landed on the continent and journeyed towards the South Pole to reach 80°S, and carried out some exploration of King Edward VII Land. While the Norwegian foreign ministry never really used Amundsen's claiming in a legal sense, it did give symbolic depth to Norway's claims. Japan was forced to renounce any claims to polar territory in the aftermath of the Second World War.

The Terra Nova Expedition (1910–13), led by Robert Scott, aimed explicitly to be the first to reach the South Pole and enjoyed the strong support of the Royal Geographical Society. The Society's president, Sir Clements Markham, was a major sponsor. Scott and his party reached the South Pole on 17 January 1912, but discovered that the rival expedition led by Roald Amundsen had triumphed some 33 days earlier. Scott confided to his diary that, 'The Pole. Yes, but under very different circumstances from those expected . . . Great God! This is an awful place and terrible enough for us to have laboured to it without the reward of priority.'

On their return journey, despite initially enjoying reasonable weather and decent progress, the five-strong party encountered difficulties, including physical disintegration due to frostbite and malnutrition. Assailed by ferociously cold weather, sledging became akin to 'pulling over desert sand'. With shortages of food and fuel, one member of the party, Captain Lawrence 'Titus' Oates, sacrificed himself for the sake of the remaining three, after the early death of Evans. The final three, Scott, Wilson, and Bowers, trudged on and made it to 11 miles short of their main depot before a blizzard prevented further progress. Their bodies, journals, and other items, including rock specimens, were discovered some eight months later.

Scott's diary dated 29 March 1912

Every day we have been ready to start for our depot *11 miles* away, but outside the door of the tent it remains a scene of whirling drift. I do not think we can hope for any better things now. We shall stick it out to the end, but we are getting weaker, of course, and the end cannot be far. It seems a pity but I do not think I can write more. R. Scott. For God's sake look after our people.

As every British school child knows, or certainly did when I was growing up in the 1970s, the final Scott expedition, while tragic, was also truly heroic. Whereas the Norwegians, familiar with the demands of the high latitudes, used dogs and seasoned Arctic clothing, Scott stood accused by his critics, some time after his untimely demise, of being too rooted in inappropriate strategies such as man-hauling and a commitment to scientific investigation. Damningly, for some at least, his party even at their darkest hour never jettisoned their interest in scientific investigation. Antarctic science, while in its infancy, was a powerful spur to further exploration, and Scott's party were interested in terrestrial magnetism, oceanography, geology, and palaeontology. Other members of Scott's expedition made extensive journeys for geological and ornithological purposes, one party enduring -70°C for the sake of collecting geological specimens and/or retrieving Emperor Penguin eggs. While an egg hunt may sound absurd, given it was not Easter and they were not made of chocolate, the penguin eggs were contributing to scientific debates about global evolution. Charles Darwin's *On the Origin of Species* (1859) was read avidly by Scott's party, and as one member, Apsley Cherry-Gerrard, noted, 'We were witnessing a marvel of the natural world. We had within our grasp material which might prove of the utmost importance to science; we were turning theories into facts with every observation we made.'

5. Robert Falcon Scott and members of his Terra Nova Expedition of 1910–13 at the South Pole in Antarctica in January 1912; Scott, at right, and his party find Amundsen's tent at the South Pole, 19 January 1912

The legacy of the Scott expedition was profound. Scientifically, the Terra Nova Expedition with its multiple parties, including the less well-known Northern Party and Western geological parties, contributed greatly to the sum of human knowledge. Politically, notwithstanding the disappointment of being eclipsed by a Norwegian team, the Antarctic was appropriated for the imperial portfolio. Photographs, along with maps and charts, played their part in establishing proof of arrival and subsequent departure. In the aftermath of the First World War, this continued apace, with the Antarctic being ever more visualized as appropriated imperial territory, and pictures of imperial heroes such as Titus Oates being shown to British troops serving in the trenches in Europe. Economically, the expedition reaffirmed the resource value of the region, and helped to fire speculation about future mineral-based wealth. Finally, and most significantly, the loss of Scott and his party – disseminated through surviving diaries, photographs, and the films of Herbert Ponting – helped to cement in the British and wider imagination a vision of tragic heroic figures battling against the odds, enriched by a dedication to duty and to one another.

Stung by this loss, coinciding as it did with another icy disaster involving the passenger ship the *RMS Titanic*, the British government and public played their part in ensuring that the Heroic Age of Antarctic exploration was commemorated solemnly. A subsequent filmic treatment starring John Mills in *Scott of the Antarctic* (1948) reinforced for post-war audiences the stoical achievements of Scott and his final party, and interestingly used still shots from the Antarctic Peninsula, and members of the Falkland Islands Dependencies Survey (FIDS) were expected to dress up and reconstruct Scott and his party's man-hauling exploits.

After the Heroic Age (1918–40)

After the Scott–Amundsen saga, there were no further journeys to the South Pole until the 1950s. Shackleton's Imperial Trans-Antarctic Expedition (1914) floundered due to his ship

Endurance being trapped in the icy waters of the Weddell Sea. Considered to be the last expedition of the Heroic Age, it was notable for its feats of 'endurance' rather than the planned trans-continental trek. Beset by ice in the Weddell Sea, Shackleton and his party of 28 men were stranded on the pack ice in the winter season of 1915. Their ship sunk after being crushed by the ice, and the men had to endure the Antarctic winter in a series of makeshift camps, surviving on remaining food stores and captured animals. Shackleton took a decision to use the lifeboats in order to journey to Elephant Island to the north of the Weddell Sea. He left the bulk of the expedition there and, together with his five companions, sailed 800 nautical miles in an open boat (the *James Baird*) to South Georgia. Once there, they clambered over the mountains and reached a Norwegian whaling community. The remaining men were eventually rescued, without any loss of life. This remains one of the 'greatest escapes' from the Antarctic.

European- and North American-sponsored Antarctic exploration, after the hiatus caused by the First World War, resumed with new interventions in ship-based, and more notably air-based, discovery. For others such as Argentina, their personnel continued to occupy a research station in the South Shetlands, and had done so continuously since 1904 after being bequeathed the base by the Scots explorer William Bruce. By way of contrast, the British invented a 'Discovery Committee' to explicitly strengthen imperial control over the Antarctic via polar science.

Established in 1923, as a result of a recommendation by the Inter-Departmental Committee on Research and Development for the Falkland Islands Dependencies (FID), the committee was charged with two inter-related tasks. First, to provide accurate and up-to-date maps and charts of the FID; and second, to assist the whaling industry with the collection of information regarding stock size and meteorology so that it could manage whaling rather than being primarily an aid to the whalers themselves. Given that whaling licences were an invaluable source of income to the FID, it was in the interest of the British government as well as the industry to ensure its longer-term sustainability. The net result was to encourage a series of survey voyages designed to study the oceanography of the Southern Ocean. During this period, the polar continent was circumnavigated, and extensive mapping was carried out around the scattered islands of South Georgia, the South Orkneys, and the South Shetlands. This was Britain's 'South Atlantic Empire'.

At the same time as the British authorities were generating information about British Antarctic waters and their major inhabitant, the whale, there was also a co-ordinated, if modestly funded, push to consolidate geographical discovery in other parts of the imperial Antarctic. Science, exploration, and empire were again being brought together to invoke, on the one hand, imperial authority and, on the other hand, a form of 'environmental authority', which entailed British administrators managing the marine life of the Southern Ocean for the benefit of humankind.

Flying over the Antarctic

While ships and sledges dominated the first hundred years of Antarctic exploration and discovery, the introduction of the aeroplane (and later the helicopter) was significant. The flight path began to supplement the sledge track. In November 1928, the Australian aviator Hubert Wilkins introduced the aircraft into Antarctic Peninsula exploration. Armed with a newspaper deal from William Randolph Hearst, Wilkins took a Lockheed Vega monoplane equipped with pontoons to the Antarctic, and created an improvised landing strip at Deception Island. On 20 December 1928, Wilkins flew for 11 hours across the Antarctic Peninsula, covering some 1,600 miles and travelling below 71°S. Recalling his land-based struggles as a young polar explorer, he revelled in what the plane offered: 'I had a tremendous feeling of power and freedom – I felt liberated. For the first time in history, new land was being discovered from the air.'

Within five years, planes and pilots were being deployed in other expeditions involving Douglas Mawson and the Norwegian Hjalmar Riiser-Larsen, who each laid the groundwork for their respective national territorial claims. The American explorer Lincoln Ellsworth made multiple expeditions between 1933 and 1939, including the first flight across the Antarctic. A contemporary of his, Admiral Richard Byrd, played his part in utilizing the aircraft to considerable effect with regard to exploration. Byrd, after establishing a base (Little America) at the Bay of Whales in January 1929, used his Ford tri-motor aircraft, the *Floyd Bennett*, to undertake the first ever flight to the South Pole. In November 1929, the pilot and passengers reached the spot where Amundsen and Scott had visited nearly 20 years earlier. As Byrd noted, 'There was nothing now to mark that scene; only a white desolation and solitude disturbed by the sound of our engines.' With favourable flying weather, the plane could conduct extensive reconnaissance flights, and explore vast swathes of previously unsighted territory. It could and did eclipse the achievements of land-based expeditions, and a new generation of polar explorers were being fêted for their aeronautical endurance as opposed to their handling of snow and dogs. The Antarctic map was transformed again, as new geographical features were identified from the air, and subsequently named after explorers and sponsors alike.

The British Graham Land Expedition (1934–7), under the leadership of John Rymill, used aircraft to help demonstrate that the Antarctic Peninsula was physically connected to the rest of the polar continent. Using a De Havilland Fox Moth reconnaissance plane, equipped with floats and skis, the team explored the southern Antarctic Peninsula region, which was poorly mapped and barely visited in comparison to the northern tip. Twenty years later, the British government invested in the aerial mapping of the Peninsula region via the Falkland Islands Dependencies Aerial Survey Expedition (FIDASE, 1955–7), which was carried out by the Hunting Aerosurveys. Canso planes, imported from Arctic

Canada, were used to continue the mapping and surveying of British Antarctic territories, and helicopters played a critical role in ferrying surveyors around the targeted areas.

The impact of the aeroplane in terms of Antarctic exploration was mixed. On the one hand, the plane and the pilot became a powerful expression of the modern age of exploration. Unlike the foot-slogging Edwardian explorer, the pilot could soar over the polar interior and coastline, sighting thousands of square miles of territory. The plane was an instrument of geopolitical power. British, American, and German pilots played their part in projecting the ambitions of their sponsoring states, even aiding and abetting the aerial colonization of the Antarctic by throwing flags out of the aeroplane window. And if German forces had prevailed during the Second World War, then perhaps the aerial exploits of the Neu-Schwabenland expedition would have been more strongly commemorated on the Antarctic map. On the other hand, flights could be disrupted by bad weather, poor landing options, and costly operation. The FIDASE remains a case in point, as a project beset with difficulties regarding cloud cover, fog, mist, freezing instruments, and gusting winds. Pilots and their planes were frequently grounded during the short summer season, and at least one helicopter was lost due to violent down-drafts. So flying and hovering were no panacea, and any mapping that was going to emerge in the aftermath needed reliable ground control. The plane and the pilot did not replace the land-based explorer and surveyor, all remaining dependent on ship-based support because the distances to be covered were still immense, and search-and-rescue facilities were non-existent.

Mega-discovery and permanent occupation (1940–58)

The Second World War created an exploratory impasse. Yet, even in the midst of the war, Argentine and British parties were exploring, mapping, and claiming Antarctic territories. In the post-1945 period, one dominant trend in Antarctic exploration was scale and permanency. New investment, provoked in part by explicit geopolitical agendas, led to a tranche of research stations and huts being established across the polar continent. The role of the armed forces was also notable. The Argentine and US navies were active in the logistical support of expeditions and the establishment of permanent infrastructure in the Antarctic; although in the case of Argentina, this was merely reinforcing their established permanent presence, dating from 1904. As in earlier times, hybrid expeditions, such as the one led by the American explorer Finn Ronne, carried out extensive aerial reconnaissance of the Ross Dependency, Australian Antarctic Territory, Dronning Maud Land, and Marie Byrd Land at the same time as the US Navy was completing naval operations High Jump and Wind Mill. Expeditions were, in this period, ambitious in scope and scale – 4,000 men and 12 ships were involved in High Jump.

The second noticeable trend was cooperation. While there was geopolitical competition in the disputed Antarctic Peninsula involving rival claimants Argentina, Chile, and the UK, there was also collaboration. In 1949, the Norwegian-British-Swedish Expedition (NBSX) introduced the world to the first multi-national example of such cooperation in the Antarctic. For two seasons, the parties attached to the NBSX carried out air surveys of Dronning Maud Land and significant glaciological research on the Antarctic's ice sheets. Following in the footsteps of that venture was the private Trans-Antarctic Expedition (1955–8) led by Vivian Fuchs, and the conqueror of Everest, Sir Edmund Hillary, involving Australian, British, New Zealand, and South African personnel. Billed as a Commonwealth enterprise combining exploration with serious science, the team used motorized tractors to cross the Antarctic continent and thus complete a journey planned by British explorers some 40 years earlier. Unfortunately for the organizers, notwithstanding the successful completion of the crossing in March 1958, the

6. The Trans-Antarctic Expedition arrives at Scott Base. The expedition, which was the first to cross Antarctica by land, was led by Sir Vivian Fuchs and Sir Edmund Hillary

expedition is remembered as much for the public falling out between Fuchs and Hillary over the nature of the crossing. A regrettable ending to a journey encompassing 2,180 miles and completed within 99 days.

Collaboration and cooperation were here to stay in the context of Antarctic exploration and investigation. During the International Geophysical Year (IGY), the Americans and New Zealanders jointly administered Hallett station. The United States also worked with Argentina and Australia, two large claimant states, in manning Wilkes and Ellsworth stations, respectively. Results were shared more readily within and beyond the scientific community, and all IGY parties accepted, albeit sometimes grudgingly, that the Antarctic was now a place of shared endeavour and enterprise.

The third trend was visualization. Ever since the earliest explorers, the Antarctic had been recorded in a variety of ways, especially by photography and film-making in the 19th and early 20th centuries. Aerial photos were, in the period between the 1930s and 1950s, vital to expeditions as proof that the polar continent and surrounding ocean were being explored, mapped, and potentially administered. Getting the photographs published and publicized was a priority for publicly and privately funded expeditions alike. Expedition leaders were expected to write articles, books, and newspaper stories highlighting their achievements to domestic and international audiences. Until somewhat eclipsed by space exploration, the Antarctic was as remote as the Moon for most people, barely visited and barely understood.

The final trend worth noting is the Cold War itself. Exploration and discovery became increasingly politicized in the 1940s and 1950s, especially when the Soviet Union resumed its interest in the Antarctic. The claimant states, including the United Kingdom and the largest of the group of seven, Australia, had to come to terms with the fact that previous episodes of exploration and discovery did not guarantee claims to ownership. The decision of the Soviet Union to re-activate its Antarctic interests in the run-up to the IGY effectively ensured the unsettling of the territorial *status quo*. In January 1958, recognizing that the Soviet Union and the United States were not going to accept their collective claims, the Macmillan government and its Australian and New Zealand counterparts realized that a roll-call of distinguished acts of Antarctic exploration was not going to suffice. Nor was permanent occupation and research station distribution. A new political settlement would have to be negotiated in the aftermath of the exploratory era.

Gendering discovery (c. 18th century onwards)

Thus far, all the acts of discovery carried out in the Antarctic were by men, and in the main, men from the Euro-American world. In her delightful short story *Sur*, the American writer Ursula Le Guin constructs a counter-factual history of Antarctica. She posits the idea that the South Pole was actually discovered by a group of South American grandmothers who arrive some months before any male explorers, including Amundsen and Scott. Their voyage is not premised on conquest, national prestige, and/or a race to some geographical point. In so doing, she reminds us that the histories of Antarctic discovery and exploration are gendered, racialized, nationalized, and civilized. The Antarctic performs as a kind of fantasy space for white European men, in particular, to perform 'firsts' and record their 'achievements' in the name of national and individual power. In *The Left Hand of Darkness*, involving a black man and an androgynous extra-terrestrial pulling Scott's sledge across a planet called 'winter', Le Guin asks us to mull over what difference it might make to the history of polar exploration if the protagonists were not assumed to be white, male, and, almost certainly, heterosexual.

Women were not encouraged for a variety of reasons, including a perceived lack of physical endurance. Expedition leaders and their managers also expressed concern that women might unsettle the routine of base life and expect separate sleeping and toilet facilities. The routine and rhythm of the intensely homo-social life of the Antarctic base faced a gendered assault. The first woman, Caroline Mikkelsen, did not set foot on the Antarctic until February 1935, and only did so because she was the partner of a Norwegian captain in command of a whaling vessel. The first women to winter over in the Antarctic were Edith Ronne and Jennie Darlington who spent a year (1947–8) in the Antarctic Peninsula with their husbands, as part of the privately organized Ronne Antarctic Research Expedition. In October 1957, two Pan-American Airlines flight attendants, Patricia Hepinstall and Ruth Kelly, working on a commercial flight over the Antarctic, landed at McMurdo Base. In 1960–1, the accomplished Australian artist Nel Law accompanied her husband Philip Law to Antarctica. The opportunities for women to discover the Antarctic were limited, however, and would remain so for decades.

When Ernest Shackleton was asked about the possible participation of women, he replied that there were 'no vacancies for the opposite sex on the Expedition'. His view was in no way unique or unusual. If there was an accompanying ideology to polar exploration, it was informed as much by gender as it was by geopolitics, science, and empire. While men may have performed gendered tasks such as cleaning and cooking within research stations and huts, they did so safe in the knowledge that everyone took their turns away from the gaze of any women – thus avoiding emasculation of sorts. And only the British, as far as I know, relished a cross-dressing party during the winter solstice – having female colleagues watching would, I suspect, have made said participants look a little silly. By way of contrast, Norwegian expeditions had designated cooks, and did not pack women's clothing in their knapsacks. Or so I have been told.

Nonetheless, women performed a variety of roles in the context of the Antarctic. While they have been physically absent from the discovery process, their presence was invoked when men were planting flags, issuing proclamations, constructing bases, and carrying out exploratory activities (claimant labour, in other words). Vast tracts of land were named after women – Marie Byrd Land, Queen Mary Land, Mount Caroline Mikkelsen. These names were submitted and approved by all-male bodies such as the US Board on Geographic Names. Women worked for government departments and organizations responsible for exploration and discovery, and later scientific programmes. In February 1999, I had the pleasure of meeting Dame Margaret Anstee, who started her career in the late 1940s in the Foreign Office working for the chief polar advisor, Dr Brian Roberts. Dame Margaret finally got to visit the Antarctic some 50 years later as a passenger on a cruise ship, after being told by her employer the Foreign Office that she was not allowed to go. More recently, Argentina and Chile have flown pregnant women down to their bases in order to strengthen their genealogical connections to the polar continent.

Scientifically, women began to make their presence felt from the 1950s onwards after overcoming prejudice and sexism within both civilian and military organizations. Women had to overcome sexist assumptions about their ability to cope with the ice, base life, and the last male bastion – the over-wintering period. But progress was slow. In 1956, a Russian marine biologist, Maria Klenova, worked in the summer station of Mirny, and, a decade later, the US finally allowed women to participate in their national programme. Women finally reached the South Pole in 1969, some fifty-odd years after men, and in the year when other men were landing on the Moon. In the 1970s, another first was achieved, this time involving the first women scientists to winter over, as part of the American Antarctic programme. It was not until the early 1990s, by way of contrast, that the British Antarctic Survey allowed women to over-winter at their stations.

The role of women in the history of Antarctic discovery remains ambivalent. On the one hand, men have dominated the Antarctic's occupation and settlement as well as exploration. Women have frequently had to battle against gendered assumptions about their suitability. On the other hand, women have been used symbolically and physically to explore, colonize, and settle the Antarctic. Women and their Antarctic children have been used for geopolitical purposes to cement national claims to territory. Both men and women, in their different ways, performed gendered service to states and sponsors. Notwithstanding the presence of women as scientists and tourists, the fact remains that men fundamentally shape the history of Antarctic exploration and engagement, those men mainly white and hailing from the Euro-American world. So there is also a racial dimension to this history of exploration. This is changing. Non-white men and a diversity of women from the global South are beginning to make their presence felt, mimicking, challenging, and extending previous acts of exploration and discovery.

Contemporary discoveries

While explorers discovered Antarctica in the sense of bringing it into systems of knowledge – such as maps (geological as well as cartographical) – it is worth also thinking of tourism as a form of discovery, this time personal rather than universal. Not mentioned in the text of the Antarctic Treaty, the omission was not surprising given that the first commercial visit occurred only in 1956 via an over-flight, and in 1957 when a Pan-American Airways aircraft landed at McMurdo Sound. For the Antarctic Treaty delegations, *les événements du jour* were science, security, and sovereignty. Within a decade of the Treaty's signing, however, ship-based cruises had become routine, usually involving yachts, even if overall numbers remained modest. Between the 1950s and 1970s, fewer than 1,000 tourists a year visited the Antarctic. Numbers began to increase in the 1980s and 1990s, with figures exceeding 5,000, and then most notably in the last decade, the figures exceeded 20,000 and peaked at 35,000–40,000 at the height of the tourist boom in the 1990s and 2000s. Following the onset of the financial crisis (c. 2008), the numbers declined somewhat to around 37,000 in 2009–10, with the vast majority voyaging by ship around the Antarctic Peninsula region, for reasons of relative proximity and cost. Many of the visitors have been women, and increasingly numbers have come from outside Europe and North America.

The tourism industry has drawn both on memories of past exploration ('In the footsteps of Scott and Shackleton') and contemporary interest in the fate of wilderness regions such as the Antarctic (a kind of disaster tourism – see it before it disappears) to dispatch far more people to the Antarctic than was possible in the years preceding the advent of the first commercial over-flight. The predominantly ship-based industry was further enhanced by the post-Cold War release of former Soviet icebreakers, which had previously worked in the Arctic region. My first visit to the Antarctic Peninsula in 1997 was on board a former Soviet Union icebreaker departing from the port of Ushuaia with only 40 passengers. The largest ships involved in Antarctic tourism, by way of contrast, were the Princess Cruise Line's *Golden Princess* and *Star Princess*, carrying more than 3,500 passengers, with more limited opportunities for actually leaving the ships once in the Antarctic.

However, the tourism industry in the Antarctic is a dynamic one. It is no longer accurately characterized as merely ship-based, with some over-flight activity. If you have the necessary resources, it is now possible to mountaineer, ski, parachute, and kayak in the Antarctic. There are far more operators compared to the early 1990s when seven operators helped to create the International Association of Antarctica Tour Operators (IAATO). By 2010–11, over 100 companies are participating, with responsibility for thousands of people sailing, landing, and flying around, in, and over the polar continent and surrounding ocean. While not all the visitors land in the Antarctic, about 27,000–28,000 people do each year. The overall value of the sector is estimated to be about US$40–50 million per year.

Discovering the Antarctic in this fashion does have costs and implications. While tourism does generate revenue for research stations selling stamps and souvenirs and can be used to help fund conservation initiatives, it can also lead to concerns about contamination of particular sites, the accidental introduction of non-indigenous species, the degradation of habitats, disruption of animal breeding, and search-and-rescue-related emergencies. In and around the Antarctic Peninsula, the twenty most popular sites are being monitored, and the sinking of the tourist-carrying *MV Explorer* in 2007 reminded the industry that accidents do happen when you 'follow in the footsteps' of past explorers (fortunately without loss of life on this occasion). The crash of Air New Zealand flight 901 in November 1979, which led to 257 people perishing when the plane struck Mount Erebus during an over-flight, remains a reminder that such activities are not risk-free. The cumulative impact of all kinds of tourism, including smaller tailor-made trips to remoter parts of the Antarctic, is still to be determined, and is difficult to ascertain given its diverse nature, albeit concentrated in the summer season.

Some members of the scientific community complain that tourism interferes with the conduct of scientific research, and can be a distraction for staff attached to research stations. Critics, however, point out that tourism in the 1980s played a powerful role in forcing scientists to improve their environmental behaviour in and around research stations. Tourists discovered that open-air burning of waste was carried out at some research stations. With the entry into force of the Protocol on Environmental Protection in 1998, Consultative Members, in consultation with IAATO, have worked to create guidelines and provisions regarding insurance, contingency planning, responsible behaviour in Antarctica, and the like. Enforcing guidelines is problematic given the contested sovereignty of Antarctica and the multi-national nature of the industry itself. Tour operators working in the Antarctic do not have to be members of IAATO, and concerns have been expressed that tour operators eager to provide their clients with ever more dramatic and extraordinary experiences will push to offer new 'discoveries' off the established routes of ship-based tourism in particular. As with skiing, there is an incentive to go off-piste, especially when faced with a situation in which you might have several ships literally taking turns to visit popular sites in the Antarctic Peninsula. Tracking and tracing vessels, in sometimes poorly mapped Antarctic waters, represents a considerable challenge made worse by commercial pressures to offer, as we noted, a unique experience. A new mandatory international code of safety for ships operating in polar waters, which might take effect in 2013, should address some outstanding concerns relating to ship safety, training, and safety equipment.

The continued discovery of Antarctica by tourists is an important element in the wider human encounter with the polar continent and surrounding ocean. There have been shipping-related accidents, and if the sector continues to expand post-financial crisis, then pressure will mount for further action regarding regulation. But we should also remember that tourism, whether invoking discovery or not, is economically and politically significant. Claimant states, especially those possessing gateway ports in Argentina, Chile, the Falkland Islands, Australia, and New Zealand, benefit from this industry. Tourists spend money in these places as well as on the boats and planes plying up and down to Antarctica. Politically, port state jurisdiction and the control of tourist activity help to cement a *de facto* authority over Antarctic territories. Argentina, Australia, and Chile have all discussed further land-based facilities such as hotels and the way in which this infrastructure provides opportunities to cement sovereign authority and make money. Tourism will never be divorced from the contested politics of Antarctica.

Summary

The history of Antarctic discovery and exploration is largely one of piecemeal coastal encounters being eclipsed by more expansive continental and subterranean exploration. As such, the Antarctic continues to surprise with new revelations about the volcanic qualities of the Southern Ocean seabed, and topographic forms under the ice sheet.

Strikingly, there remains vastly more media and indeed popular interest in tales of the physical endeavours of past European and North American explorers, usually during the 'race to the pole' era, than contemporary Antarctic discoveries. While we might admire the extraordinary bravery and tenacity of scores of explorers, scientists, and sealers, this tendency to focus on the heroic past has consequences. We tend to hear little about the way in which discovery and polar heritage is put to work by vested interests. Instead, histories of discovery are commercially exploited by tourist companies, politically exploited by governments, and intellectually exploited by authors and enthusiasts alike – tales of daring-do continue to sell.

Chapter 3
Claiming and negotiating the Antarctic

When looking at a globe, typically, the political boundaries dividing the world into 190-odd nation states will be clearly marked. There will be areas of uncertainty such as the Indo-Pakistani borderline, the status of Palestine, and/or the ownership of the Falklands/Malvinas. Looking further south, the Antarctic continent is frequently represented on globes as untroubled by political boundaries. Such a position, on the face of it, would be eminently appropriate for the only territorial region in the world without an indigenous human population. Whether by intention or omission, such globes and their representations of the political geography of the Earth are misleading. Large parts of the Antarctic are claimed by seven states – Argentina, Australia, Chile, France, New Zealand, Norway, and the United Kingdom. The most substantial claim to the polar continent is the Australian claim to Australian Antarctic Territory – some 2.2 million square miles in size – with a small, transient population. Uniquely, there is a portion of the Antarctic that is not claimed by any state and which is termed the 'unclaimed Pacific Ocean sector'.

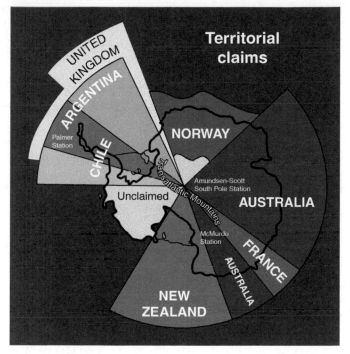

7. Territorial claims to the Antarctic

The vast majority of the international community do not accept these claims to the Antarctic. While countries such as Australia, France, New Zealand, Norway, and the United Kingdom have recognized their mutual claims, the Argentine, British, and Chilean claims overlap with one another, and the three parties remain at loggerheads. The ownership of the Antarctic remains unresolved and, just as some states believe that their claim is legitimate, other members of the international community state that this space should be considered a common property – and thus belong to all the members of the United Nations. The term 'global common' would be an appropriate description of the Antarctic.

49

Over the last hundred years, three distinct phases help to explain how the Antarctic has been claimed and colonized. This chapter tackles the claiming phase (in the main 1908–40, and epitomized by the 'Antarctic Problem'); the negotiating phase (1940s–1950s, including the International Geophysical Year and the Antarctic Treaty negotiations); and the post-colonial phase (1960s onwards). Initially, this region was immersed in colonial and anti-colonial rivalries, encompassing regional states such as Argentina, imperial states such as Britain and France, and expressly anti-colonial states such as the United States and the Soviet Union. Thereafter, on the back of major initiatives such as the International Geophysical Year (1957–8) and a US-led scientific diplomacy campaign, the 1959 Antarctic Treaty emerged after some fierce negotiations over territorial claims, nuclear testing, and the role of non-claimant states.

As a consequence of the above, the story of the Antarctic Treaty is a celebratory one. Surrounded by a series of creation myths, a vision is offered up of far-sighted men (and they are all men in this story) using science and peace to construct said landmark agreement, designed to save the Antarctic from the grubby Cold War and colonial geopolitics. Intrinsic to this rendering of events, without the complication of an indigenous population, is a benign interpretation of the immediate decades leading up to the Antarctic Treaty. It ignores the manner in which the Antarctic was colonized and administered. The role of the United States is seminal, especially in the way that it negotiated open and unfettered access to the Antarctic. Without the need for territorial colonization, the Antarctic Treaty helped to secure US dominance and Soviet interests.

Claiming phase

Notwithstanding a lack of an indigenous human population, the Antarctic was colonized by a variety of imperial powers and post-colonial states over a period of some 500 years. The

Columbian encounter with the so-called New World initiated this colonizing process. Under the terms of the Treaty of Tordesillas (1494) and an earlier Bull Inter-Caetera (1493), Spain claimed title to all territory west of a line extending from the Arctic to the Antarctic. On the eve of their respective independence, Argentina and Chile believed that they inherited those territorial rights to the same areas of the Spanish Empire. As with their continental territories, a major question confronting these newly created post-colonial states was where their mutual boundary might lie stretching from the northern Andes to the South Pole.

Argentine and Chilean national histories are taken up with the demarcation of an international boundary and the resolution of disputed territories in the Andean borderlands. Both states extend their national territories southwards, and in the case of Argentina, the so-called 'Conquest of the Desert' in the 1880s decimated indigenous peoples. By the turn of the 19th century, negotiations were ongoing over the extreme south such as Tierra del Fuego and the Beagle Channel into Drake's Passage, where the mutual boundary was fuzzy but it would extend to the South Pole. These claims to a southerly frontier were open-ended, vaguely defined, and implicit but not insignificant. Argentina was the first country in the world to maintain a permanent presence in the Argentine Antarctic sector.

Audaciously, at least to South Americans, the UK issued a defined claim to the Antarctic in 1908 via Letters Patent. Revised again in 1917, the British claim to the Falkland Islands Dependencies (FID) extended the South Atlantic Empire southwards following the annexation of the Falkland Islands in the 1830s. Spurred on by whaling and further acts of discovery and exploration, the British established a series of legal, political, and scientific mechanisms and procedures designed to consolidate imperial control. Leopold Amery, who served as Colonial Secretary from 1924 to 1929 and advocated British imperial authority throughout his long career, was at the forefront of endeavours to extend British control over the whole of the Antarctic, even if it was only partially mapped and explored. Invoking 'environmental authority', British officials opined that the UK was uniquely blessed with scientific and administrative skills necessary to manage a challenging piece of real estate, with whales that needed careful management.

Pursuing this 'selfless' policy, British officials encouraged New Zealand to assume administration of the Ross Dependency in 1923, and Australia to lay claim to an enormous sector called the Australian Antarctic Territory. South Africa was approached as well, but declined to actively help the Antarctic turn pink on British imperial maps. In response to British imperial manoeuvrings, France announced that it would claim another part of the Antarctic, on the basis of past acts of exploration and discovery, especially by the 19th-century explorer Jules Dumont d'Urville. In 1924, the French territory of Adélie Land was established, and extended sector-like towards the South Pole. Significantly, the French claim was later recognized by Britain, Australia, and New Zealand. Amery's master plan for total imperial control was thwarted, though dreams of almost-complete British control persisted. Britain really did not want any neighbours in the Antarctic.

In the same year of the French claim, the United States, under its Secretary of State Charles Hughes, emphasized an 'open-door' policy for the Antarctic, unrestricted by the territorial claiming by others. Significantly, this declaration brought to the fore two competing visions for the Antarctic. On the one hand, claimant states were eager to delineate their national/imperial spheres, while claiming to be acting on behalf of 'mankind'. On the other, the US represented a different vision, one less motivated by territorial claiming (at least publicly) and more by open access.

Up and until the late 1930s, territorial claiming prevailed. Norway, in advance of a feared territorial claim by the German Antarctic (Neu-Schwabenland) Expedition, announced that they would be laying claim to a sector of the Antarctic between the Falkland Islands Dependencies and the Australian Antarctic Territory. Termed 'Dronning Maud Land', the Norwegian claim was based on previous whaling expeditions in the region, and was formally announced on 14 January 1939. At the same time, however, German aluminium markers embossed with swastika lay abandoned over the ice-bound coast, in what the German (rather than any Norwegian) expedition leaders termed 'Neuschwabenland'. Germany's defeat in 1945 ended hopes of a German Antarctic sector, but did not dampen speculation that some Nazis still dreamed of resurrecting a Fourth Reich there. Japan, too, forfeited any claim, despite earlier involvement in exploration and whaling.

Argentina (claim made in 1940) and Chile (claim made in 1943) were late starters by European standards. Unlike the others, they were convinced that their southerly territories were part of an imperial inheritance and integral to national territories. The only issue to be resolved was the declaration of a mutual boundary between two South American neighbours. In that sense, there was no Argentine or Chilean *claim*. Argentina and Chile copied the behaviour of Britain, mindful of international legal precedents regarding remote and thinly occupied spaces. In mimicking the behaviour of an imperial state, Argentine and Chilean parties participated in their own ceremonies of possession, usually involving planting flags, reading solemn declarations, mapping territory, assessing resources, and naming places after independence heroes such as Bernardo O'Higgins and José de San Martín.

Britain hoped vainly that the US might claim the hitherto unwanted Pacific Ocean sector and join the claimant club – not unreasonably given that US Antarctic expeditions in the 1930s and 1940s carried out 'sovereignty performances' such as dropping flags out of aeroplane windows. Furthermore, Richard Byrd reported back to his political masters about evidence of mineral wealth of the polar continent in a blatant attempt to stimulate further interest. Later, he even posited the idea of setting off nuclear explosions to melt the ice and reveal all those would-be minerals – a form of nuclear engineering. However, US reluctance to make a claim was critical in shaping the future politics of the Antarctic, and for the intervening years added extra uncertainty for the claimant club's membership. Their reaction was to devise new roles and rules in order to fix, map, and record their presence – a new round of 'sovereignty games' was unleashed on the Antarctic.

Sovereignty games and the Antarctic Problem

In 1943–4, in the midst of the Second World War, British troops and scientists were dispatched to the Antarctic, in a secret naval operation called Operation Tabarin. Named after a Parisian nightclub, and backed by Prime Minister Churchill, the aim was straightforward. British personnel were expected to strengthen Britain's title to the territory in question, and this meant establishing a permanent foothold. Bases were created, flags were raised, plaques were secured, post offices established, theodolites were readied, and signposts embossed with 'crown lands' were planted. Britain was getting serious – pressing surveys into action and busily issuing postage stamps. It was going to be a policy of *terra nostra* rather than *mare nostrum*.

In 1951, a British civil servant, Bill Hunter Christie, published an insightful book called *The Antarctic Problem*. From his vantage point of the British Embassy in Buenos Aires, Hunter Christie was well placed to record the growing agitation surrounding the overlapping claims of Argentina, Chile, and the United Kingdom. Coincidentally, this Antarctic agitation sat uneasily with a growing British dependence on Argentine meat supplies in a post-war period of rationing. UK economic interests in Argentina were also under scrutiny by nationalist governments in Argentina, especially under the leadership of Juan Domingo Perón.

All three countries were entrenching their Antarctic claims within public culture by commemorating, educating, drawing, and studying the Antarctic Peninsula and surrounding islands. In Argentina and Chile, a new generation of citizens was weaned on new geography textbooks detailing how Antarctic territories were geographically and geologically connected to South America. Just as the 19th century witnessed patriotic forms of education in South America, post-war Argentines and Chileans were learning that their countries did not stop at the southern point of the South American continent. In contrast, a generation of British school children (as a special treat) got to see John Mills star as Robert Falcon Scott in Ealing Studios' *Scott of the Antarctic* (1948) in the cinema. In their varying ways, children in three different countries were learning that the Antarctic was part of their national experience, either as integral territory or as a staging ground for national interests and values.

Frustrated by this continuing and expensive 'Antarctic Problem', the United Kingdom submitted an application to the International Court of Justice (ICJ) in May 1955 asking 'the Court to recognise the validity of its titles to sovereignty and to declare that the pretentions of Argentina and Chile, as well as their encroachments in those territories, are contrary to international law'. The territories in this case referred to all British territories south of 50th parallel of south latitude. The application never attracted the involvement of the counter-claimants because both rejected the need to have their 'claims' tested by an international court. If they had participated, then they would have been obliged to abide by any ICJ judgment. With no judgment, the 'Antarctic Problem' persisted, with all three countries devoting resources to the protection, and indeed enhancement, of their respective territories. Argentina, in particular, was a polar superpower dispatching icebreakers, planes, and personnel to the Antarctic Peninsula. Argentine officials took great pleasure in sending updated maps of the Argentine Antarctic Territory to British administrators which highlighted their surveying achievements.

The ICJ application was only one element in the contested sovereignty of the Antarctic. The United States, having renewed its Antarctic commitments and interests in the late 1940s, assembled a decisive presence. On the back of a new generation of US Navy-led expeditions, State Department officials explored governance options with the polar G7 (the claimant states). Given the intra-gang rivalries, any proposal to alter the *status quo* was likely to encounter hostility at worst and indifference at best.

Mindful of the potential to make a substantial claim to the Antarctic, a proposal for a condominium was carefully considered by the claimants in 1948. Within such a condominium, the United States hoped to achieve three things. First, to ensure that its rights and interests were preserved across the entire polar continent as well as protecting navigation rights/rights of innocent passage around the Southern Ocean. Second, successive US governments were concerned about the unresolved tension between Britain, Argentina, and Chile. From the US perspective, three Cold War allies locked into an increasingly bitter dispute over ownership with no sign that any of those parties were willing to 'pull out' of the Antarctic made no sense. Finally, it was hoped that other parties, especially the Soviet Union, might be discouraged from playing a more prominent role in the Antarctic if affairs of state appeared benign. In other words, the US was prepared to deal with the seven claimants in the hope that they could shut down the Antarctic politically.

This proposed management strategy failed. It assumed that the Soviet Union was preoccupied with its vast Arctic region. The return of whaling fleets coupled with the promotion work of Soviet geographers scuppered the plan. Sensing growing Soviet interest, the American and British media foretold of a new 'scramble for Antarctica'. By 1950, Soviet officials asserted their historic and geographical interest in the Antarctic, and publicly refuted the validity of any territorial claims to the Antarctic. As with the United States, the USSR adopted a non-recognition policy while reserving the right to press a claim in the future. The subsequent investment in scientific initiatives fitted a broader pattern of both countries being avowedly anti-imperial, while at the same time supporting proposals that ensured that their influence (and mobility in the case of the Antarctic) was at best enhanced and, at very worst, untouched.

Indirectly, perhaps, a proposal put forward in 1950 by a group of geophysicists for a new international polar year (the International Geophysical Year, IGY) was a timely intervention. Polar science offered a powerful platform for geopolitical advantage, and just as the British utilized it in the 1920s and 1930s, claims could be made to be advancing 'environmental authority' and material interests simultaneously. Big science provided opportunities for both colonization/sovereignty games, and paradoxically perhaps, shared ownership.

Negotiating phase

Following on from earlier international polar years in 1882–3 and 1932–3, plans were hatched for an International Geophysical Year (1957–8). The origins of the IGY owe much to the scientific interests of two distinguished scientists, James Van Allen and Sydney Chapman. The IGY was conceived as a major initiative to collect synoptic information and enhance understanding of planet Earth and the solar system. Van Allen and Chapman were not interested in the contested politics of Antarctica, but the polar regions were an area of importance for IGY planners. As such, the Antarctic was no longer considered a strange and remote place on the margins of world affairs; rather, it was viewed as an essential component of the Earth's geophysical condition.

An international committee, the Special Committee for the IGY, was created, and some 67 countries committed themselves to global scientific investigation. In the period between July 1957 and December 1958, particular attention was to be given to the polar regions and outer space. With Cold War tensions evident in the Arctic region, the Antarctic enjoyed prominence, in contrast to earlier international polar years. The preparatory meetings leading up to the IGY established the 'ground rules'. In 1955, it was agreed that Antarctic research had to be carried out on the basis that sovereignty considerations were separated from scientific investigation. Twelve nations, including the seven claimants, participated, and some 5,000 personnel at 55 research stations carried out a range of investigations, including the mapping of the Antarctic, ice-cap thickness studies, marine biology, and upper atmospheric research.

Claimant states had to accept that the Americans and Soviets were going to establish their bases across the region, including an American one at the South Pole and a Soviet research station at the Pole of Relative Inaccessibility. Both superpowers were making a powerful political and symbolic point – claimants had no special rights in the context of international scientific investigation. The scientific station offered a new model of colonization – whereas claimant states created research stations as part of their national strategies, other non-claimants such as Japan were able to point to IGY scientific priorities and suggest, more plausibly perhaps, that they were acting in the interests of 'mankind'. Rhetorically speaking, 'scientific authority' was replacing 'environmental authority', and claimant states needed to accept not only trespassing but also encampment.

While the IGY generated extraordinary amounts of new data on the Antarctic, including on the upper atmosphere, it created compelling precedents. Science could be a powerful mechanism for international cooperation, while scientists relished having unfettered access to the continent and surrounding ocean. Scientific bases, while information-processing colonies, also provided a visible manifestation of claimant and non-claimant interest in the Antarctic. New stations sprang up all over the continent and surrounding islands. Britain, for example, established a new base at

Halley Bay, and the three counter-claimants managed to collaborate with one another in the Antarctic Peninsula region. Australia had to accept that Soviet bases in the Australian Antarctic Territory could not be wished away. Finally, the IGY offered a possible scientific-diplomatic model for the future governance of the Antarctic. Could the parties be persuaded to continue to cooperate with one another even if the sovereignty of the Antarctic remained unsettled? What would happen after the IGY – would there be a new 'scramble for the Antarctic'?

These questions were pressed in newspapers and magazines around the world. In the midst of the IGY and beyond, the United States hosted a series of meetings with the IGY Antarctic parties in the hope that there might be some modicum of agreement over arrangements post-December 1958. Nothing was certain at this stage. While the IGY was extended by a further year in order to continue with a range of scientific endeavours, some of the claimants, including Argentina, Australia, and Britain, were uneasy about the enduring presence of the US and Soviet Antarctic programmes in 'their' territories. Australian commentators hoped that the 'Reds' would leave their 'bit' of the Antarctic. While Argentina and Chile worried about the Americans, all parties accepted Japan's presence. Both superpowers, by the end of the IGY, were adamant that they were not 'departing' the Antarctic. A ring of scientific stations transformed the international politics of the Antarctic.

So if the path towards the Antarctic Treaty was decisively shaped by the experiences of the IGY, it was not a straightforward one. Britain and its Commonwealth allies were still eager for the Soviet Union to be excluded from any future political arrangement. Argentina and Chile were deeply troubled by the precedent set by the IGY in allowing unfettered access to their territories. Norway was more preoccupied with the Arctic, and uncertain about its long-term commitment, but reluctant to lose face. New Zealand, mindful of the substantial US presence in its Ross Dependency, even contemplated renouncing its territorial claim. Any agreement was likely to involve signing up to some kind of framework guaranteeing unrestricted access and recognition that others might, at some later date, press a claim to the Antarctic. This was a bitter pill to swallow for the gang of seven.

While science was perfectly capable of being put to work in ways that exceeded the selfless pursuit of knowledge creation and exchange, polar science was also colonizing the Antarctic, and generating new expectations, conventions, procedures, and rules. The IGY brought into sharper focus a different kind of geophysical and geopolitical architecture – one based on recognizing that the Antarctic was an integral part of planet Earth and its geophysical systems. As such, it offered a different vision, one that was potentially far removed from the contest between nations for defined sovereign rights.

Post-colonial Antarctica

The signing of the Antarctic Treaty on 1 December 1959, negotiated between the United States and eleven other parties including Britain and the Soviet Union, was far from a smooth process. Having gathered in October 1959, on the back of an invitation from the US State Department to those countries involved in the Antarctic dimension of the IGY, the omens were not good. Even after some 60 preliminary meetings, the twelve parties disagreed with one another over some fundamental issues. The most significant was the question of ownership. The seven claimant states, with the partial exception of resource-strapped New Zealand, were determined to retain their claimant gang membership. Every head of delegation to the claimant states devoted their opening addresses to articulating their 'inalienable' rights to, at least a portion of, the continent. For the five other parties, including Belgium, Japan, and South Africa, these words were emblematic of wishful thinking. For the last decade, the United States and the Soviet Union had refused to recognize any sovereign rights to the Antarctic, and what is more, reiterated their right to press their own claims in the future. The IGY did nothing to alter this worldview; rather, it reinforced it.

For all the IGY and its fine rhetoric, sovereignty and ownership of the Antarctic was a stumbling block. There were also additional problems to be confronted – since members of the armed forces supported the IGY scientists, did the Antarctic need to be demilitarized? The US Navy was the biggest operator under its annual Operation Deep Freeze programme, and if other militaries implemented further exercises, they might resuscitate former tensions. Should nuclear testing be banned given that the continent was free from indigenous human population? One could argue that it was better to test there than on supposedly thinly populated areas in the Pacific Ocean and Siberia. Was it reasonable for other signatories to demand the right of inspection of other scientific stations and installations in order to ensure that the content and spirit of any nascent treaty was respected? Could there be an 'open-skies' policy in the Antarctic whereby parties could observe one another from the air? How would one enforce any measures if sovereignty were disputed? Did the parties concerned need to discuss resource-related issues such as mining and/or fishing? Would scientists and science be sufficiently emollient to overcome schisms of the future? And, whatever the answers to these questions and more, this conference was planned for 1959 – the year, as it turned out, of the Cuban revolution.

With the help of the neatly typed diaries of Brian Roberts, a senior member of the British delegation to the Antarctic Treaty conference, we gain some insights into the febrile atmosphere (and his personality type). As he confided:

> It is not possible to continue this record in the way I hoped.... What spare time I can find is spent drafting telegrams for the Foreign Office or preparing memoranda for Sir Esler [Head of the British Delegation]. These are usually finished by about half past one

or 2 o'clock in the morning and by that time I want only to go to
bed exhausted.... I wake up from a nightmare of papers suddenly
realising that I am not in the stuffy conference room.

Surrounded by potted palm trees, the delegation including Roberts
knew that some kind of political-legal-scientific settlement was
vital. The Cubans had their revolution; now the Antarctic needed
one. As a claimant state, austerity-weakened Britain had invested
hundreds of thousands of pounds in creating and sustaining a
scientific and logistical programme designed to keep at bay two
South American rival claimants – Argentina and Chile. But the
South American states were never going to drop their 'claims' to
the Antarctic Peninsula region. Unlike Britain, the South American
states were not managing a diminishing imperial portfolio, some of
which was problematic, and were not embroiled in defence
commitments around the world from Korea to West Germany. The
British Treasury was demanding savings, and Roberts and the
team needed a formula with the imprimatur of the United States
that would be both cost-saving and face-saving. Failure to find
some kind of international agreement would lead to Antarctic
withdrawal. In 1958, the Treasury made it clear to the Foreign
Office and Colonial Offices that further investment was not going
to be sanctioned to defend a remote and uninhabited part of the
British Empire with questionable resource value.

All the participants brought their own agendas regarding a
possible settlement. For the Soviets, for example, simply
participating was significant given earlier attempts by the seven
claimant states and the United States to try and exclude them
from shaping the future governance of the Antarctic. The Soviet
delegation was determined to ensure that their non-recognition
policy of existing claims was respected and was eager that the
region be demilitarized, especially given American plans (however
tentative) to consider the possibility of nuclear testing. The
southern hemispheric states such as Argentina and Australia were
deeply concerned about nuclear testing and covert submarine

activities in the Southern Ocean. Smaller countries such as Belgium and Norway were eager to be represented even if, in the case of Norway, the Euro-Arctic region was a more pressing priority. Finally, for *apartheid* South Africa, this was a major international meeting in which the white minority government could take its place without fear of isolation.

The conference closed in late November with the Antarctic Treaty open for signature on 1 December 1959. The treaty applies to all areas south of 60° south latitude. The preamble of the treaty establishes its genealogical record and future-orientated goals:

> *Recognizing* that it is in the interest of all mankind that Antarctica shall continue for ever to be used exclusively for peaceful purposes and shall not become the scene or object of international discord;
>
> *Acknowledging* the substantial contributions to scientific knowledge resulting from international cooperation in scientific investigation in Antarctica;
>
> *Convinced* that the establishment of a firm foundation for the continuation and development of such cooperation on the basis of freedom of scientific investigation in Antarctica as applied during the International Geophysical Year accords with the interests of science and the progress of all mankind;
>
> *Convinced* also that a treaty ensuring the use of Antarctica for peaceful purposes only and the continuance of international harmony in Antarctica will further the purposes and principles embodied in the Charter of the United Nations.

The reference to the Charter of the United Nations is noteworthy as twelve nations invoked the assumed authority of the 'international community', including countries such as India that raised the 'question of Antarctica' in 1956 and 1958 at the UN. The Indian interventions played their part in reminding the negotiating parties that interest in the Antarctic was growing, especially in parts of the world without a lengthy record of exploratory and scientific engagement.

India and the 'question of Antarctica'

We are not challenging anybody's rights there [in Antarctica]. But it has become important that the matter be considered by the United Nations. The fact that Antarctica contains many very important minerals – especially atomic energy minerals – is one reason why this area is attractive to various countries. We thought it would be desirable to have a discussion about this in the United Nations.

Prime Minister Jawaharlal Nehru, 1958

The articles within the treaty outline the following commitments: the Antarctic should be used for exclusively peaceful purposes with no scope for military activities; there should be an unfettered freedom to conduct scientific research throughout the Antarctic; international scientific cooperation requires parties share their information with one another; the treaty parties agree to put to one side their disagreements over sovereignty and that by cooperating with one another it is recognized that no new and or enlarged claims can be made to the region; nuclear weapons testing, storage, and dumping is banned; an inspection system should be created to ensure compliance; and measures are put in place to ensure that the parties can resolve disputes, and meet again to consider supplementary additions to the treaty and associated instruments. Mindful of the fact that nobody wanted to commit to this nascent treaty in perpetuity, a clause was included to enable a possible review of the treaty 30 years later, after its entry into force.

The linchpin of the treaty was Article 4. Without it, everything else would have collapsed in a proverbial heap. Article 4 stipulated the following:

1. Nothing contained in the present Treaty shall be interpreted as:
   a. A renunciation by any Contracting Party of previously asserted rights of or claims to territorial sovereignty in Antarctica;

b. A renunciation or diminution by any Contracting Party of any basis of claim to territorial sovereignty in Antarctica which it may have whether as a result of its activities or those of its nationals in Antarctica, or otherwise;

c. Prejudicing the position of any Contracting Party as regards its recognition or non-recognition of any other State's rights of or claim or basis of claim to territorial sovereignty in Antarctica.

2. No acts or activities taking place while the present Treaty is in force shall constitute a basis for asserting, supporting or denying a claim to territorial sovereignty in Antarctica or create any rights of sovereignty in Antarctica. No new claim, or enlargement of an existing claim, to territorial sovereignty in Antarctica shall be asserted while the present Treaty is in force.

In essence, the seven claimant states were not asked to either renounce or diminish their sovereign claims for the duration of the treaty. In return, however, they had to accept several things. Non-claimants such as the United States and the Soviet Union retained their right to press a claim to the Antarctic in the future. Non-claimants and claimants alike could carry out scientific research across the polar continent, and claimants such as Australia would simply have to accept the presence of Soviet bases in the Australian Antarctic Territory. Finally, everyone was expected to embrace, under the terms of Article 7, the obligations regarding inspection and advanced notification of plans to dispatch expeditions, including military personnel, to the region. So, sovereignty-related questions were treated in a deliberately ambiguous manner. This suited the superpowers. Article 4 was a subtle act of hegemonic power. There was no need, after all, for either the US or the Soviet Union to initiate an actual claim to Antarctica.

The treaty was available for signing some six weeks after the opening presentations by heads of delegations. We should acknowledge the role of restraint and absence in securing such a speedy agreement. There were very real tensions between the parties. Sovereignty was a major obstacle, and for countries such as Argentina and, to a lesser extent, Chile, the idea that the country should 'sign away' its papal inheritance was unthinkable. There was a very real danger that the Argentine delegation would simply walk away or, further down the ratification track, discover that the Argentine parliament would refuse to accede to the treaty. Argentine parliamentarians understood that the treaty was cementing the authority of the US in particular to circumvent the sovereignty politics of Antarctica. So Article 4, however clever and open-ended, was not a magic bullet in itself. It had to be negotiated and accepted within the domestic territories of the twelve states. The entry into force of the treaty was not certain on 1 December 1959 because every signatory had to confirm that accession was completed domestically. And Argentina was crucial given its claimant-state status and involvement in the most contested part of the Antarctic. All the parties, whether by design and/or accident, managed to display some form of restraint from aggressive territorial nationalism, not to mention the disciplinary constraints of Cold War antagonism.

The other factor at play here was absence. Resources were not discussed, formally at least, at the Washington Conference. In large part, this was due to the fact that the sovereignty question inevitably raised issues pertaining to the ownership of onshore and offshore resources. Unlike India, no one mobilized a view of the Antarctic as an under-exploited resource frontier. The spectre of resources was never far from those discussions, however. Public awareness of the Antarctic was far higher now, and stories alerting readers of untold riches awaiting discovery and exploitation were legion. The Antarctic's living resource potential was immense, and whaling now fell under the remit of the International Whaling Commission (established in 1946). In non-living resource terms, evidence abounded of mineral potential, even if a combination of distance, remoteness, and inaccessibility made it an unlikely short-term development. The point was as much about future possibilities and possible futures. The delegates at Washington recognized that resource use and management would have to be tackled at a later date.

Summary

The Antarctic Treaty stabilized the deeply divisive problem of territorial sovereignty. Article 4 'froze' sovereignty positions and facilitated the emergence of science to be the determining factor in shaping access to terrain and scientific data. The treaty protected the colonial *status quo ante*. Unlike in other parts of the world, it was still possible to be a good colonizer, albeit one signed up to the Antarctic Treaty. After its entry into force, all the claimant states continued to believe that their territorial claims were intact and fundamentally unchanged. Stamps continued to be issued, textbooks authored, and maps drawn proclaiming the existence of an Australian Antarctic Territory, a Chilean Antarctic Territory, a Ross Dependency, and so on.

Building on the legacy of the IGY and the Washington Conference was the next challenge for those who gathered in the autumn of 1959. The Antarctic Treaty parties, as with the British imperialists of the past, argued that their claims to scientific and environmental authority were being used in the interests of all humankind. This was a critical factor given the preservation of these territorial claims, which were stretching any reasonable test of the global good. However strategic the preamble of the treaty, some questions remained to be addressed. Could the treaty provide a foundation for further cooperation in the area of resources and environmental protection? If not, then would it endure given the territorial stakes at play? Throughout the Washington negotiations, the 'Antarctic Problem' was re-packaged rather than resolved.

Finally, the role of the United States needs to be seen for what it was. The Antarctic Treaty offers a good example of hegemonic power. There was no reason to make a claim to the Antarctic, as the United States secured the right to go anywhere and everywhere. If the treaty failed, then they had a fallback position – to press a claim to vast swathes of the polar continent on the basis of an extensive history of discovery, exploration, and settlement. Claimant states such as Britain faced a dilemma – how to administer and regulate one's territory without alienating powerful neighbours and partners? This sovereignty dilemma was more or less manageable when the parties in question numbered just twelve.

Chapter 4
Governing the Antarctic

In the midst of a worsening Cold War, the signing and entering into force of the 1959 Antarctic Treaty was a notable achievement. This treaty established a framework for the demilitarization of the Antarctic and the promotion of international cooperation, especially in the field of science. Article 4, as noted earlier, ensured that no new claims to polar territory were to be asserted while the treaty was in force. For the chief architect of the treaty, the United States, this framework was praised for 'containing all the provisions which the US believed were required for the protection of its national interest and as setting a precedent in the field of disarmament, prohibition of nuclear explosions, and the law of space'. On ratifying the treaty, American senators recognized that with the promotion of scientific cooperation, freedom of access, and peaceful usages of the Antarctic, there was no immediate need for a territorial claim.

Upon the Treaty's entry into force in June 1961, the Antarctic became the world's first nuclear-free zone, and provided inspiration for further denuclearizing initiatives elsewhere. Moreover, the treaty placed peaceful cooperation and scientific collaboration as the core business of the signatories, later to be termed Antarctic Treaty Consultative Parties (ATCPs). Governing by consensus is the *sine qua non* of those parties. Together, the treaty and subsequent instruments such as the Convention on the Conservation of Living Resources (entry into force, 1982) and the Protocol on Environmental Protection (entry into force, 1998) all make up the Antarctic Treaty System (ATS). Science is frequently described as *the* core activity, and indicative of ongoing cooperation amongst the parties, subject to no restrictions on location of activity. A constellation of agreements continues to strive to conserve, preserve, and protect the Antarctic terrestrial and marine environments.

These features explain a great deal when it comes to the longevity of the Antarctic Treaty. In the last few years, a number of events, including a high-profile Antarctic Treaty Summit hosted by the Smithsonian Institution at Washington, DC, have celebrated the capacity and willingness of Antarctic Treaty Consultative Parties to govern the Antarctic. At the joint session of the Antarctic Treaty Consultative Parties Meeting and the Arctic Council in April 2009, Secretary of State Hillary Clinton reminded her audience that:

> In 1959, representatives from 12 countries came together in Washington to sign the Antarctic Treaty, which is sometimes referred to as the first arms control agreement of the Cold War. Today, 47 nations have signed it. And as a result, Antarctica is one of the few places on earth where there has never been war. Other than occasional arguments among scientists and those stationed there over weighty matters having to do with sports, entertainment, and science, there has been very little conflict.
>
> It is a land where science is the universal language and the highest priority and where people from different regions, races, and religions live and work together in one of the planet's most remote, beautiful, and dangerous places.
>
> The genius of the Antarctic Treaty lies in its relevance today.

Most commentators reflecting on the Antarctic Treaty's 50th anniversary (either 2009 or 2011 depending on signing or entry into force respectively) concluded that this was an example of 'good governance'. The parties, on this assessment, continue to respect the spirit and content of the treaty and its associated legal instruments while maintaining a sense of accountability, openness, and a capacity to innovate in a positive sense.

In this chapter, we consider the last 50 years and reflect on how the Antarctic Treaty Consultative Parties worked to create an evolving international institutional and regime-based structure, with the aim of strengthening the original treaty. The Antarctic Treaty represents one of the most successful experiments in regional governance, albeit one in which there was no indigenous human population to contend with. Moreover, the geographical and political remoteness of the Antarctic in the 1950s and 1960s in particular aided and abetted those determined to make the Antarctic Treaty 'work'. When challenges did emerge in the 1970s and 1980s, the parties in question had, in effect, an invented tradition of regional governance to draw upon to not only resist critics but also advocate reform of the Antarctic Treaty System in areas such as membership, information exchange, as well as legal instruments such as the Protocol on Environmental Protection. Critically, this Protocol prohibits all form of mining and mineral exploitation, thus mollifying those who thought that the treaty parties were hell-bent on dividing the resource riches of the Antarctic. More recently, notwithstanding the introduction of a secretariat in 2001, there has been less willingness to negotiate new protocols for issues of growing concern such as biological prospecting and tourism. The latter may become more troubling in the future and thus demand closer attention from the treaty parties.

The Antarctic Treaty and its entry into force

With the entry into force of the Antarctic Treaty in June 1961, the governance of the Antarctic entered into a new stage.

Article 9 of the 1959 Antarctic Treaty

Representatives of the Contracting Parties named in the preamble to the present Treaty shall meet at the City of Canberra within two months after the date of entry into force of the Treaty, and thereafter at suitable intervals and places, for the purpose of exchanging information, consulting together on matters of common interest pertaining to Antarctica, and formulating and considering, and recommending to their Governments, measures in furtherance of the principles and objectives of the Treaty, including measures regarding:

a. Use of Antarctica for peaceful purposes only;
b. Facilitation of scientific research in Antarctica;
c. Facilitation of international scientific cooperation in Antarctica;
d. Facilitation of the exercise of the rights of inspection provided for in Article VII of the Treaty;
e. Questions relating to the exercise of jurisdiction in Antarctica;
f. Preservation and conservation of living resources in Antarctica.

The first Antarctic Treaty Consultative Meeting (ATCM) in Canberra initiated a new entry into the diplomatic calendar. All the parties committed themselves to meet every two years to formally consider the workings of what was later to be termed the Antarctic Treaty System (ATS). This term is widely used to describe the 1959 Antarctic Treaty plus those measures negotiated by the ATCPs under Article 9 of the treaty. This might include treaties, measures, decisions, and recommendations. While Antarctic scientists in particular would continue to meet and exchange information more frequently, the governance process was shaped by those biennial encounters – a remarkable thing in itself, and a sure sign that those addressing the Antarctic were subject to less immediate pressures. Significantly, Article 9 acknowledged that the 'preservation and conservation of living resources in Antarctica' was a topic worthy of further negotiation and possible additional measures.

Over the proceeding 50 years, four major trends emerged. First, the Antarctic Treaty was buttressed and extended by additional legal instruments addressing conservation, resource management, and environmental protection.

Legal instruments supplementing the Antarctic Treaty

1964 Agreed Measures for the Conservation for Flora and Fauna (AMCFF)

1972 Convention for the Conservation of the Antarctic Seals (CCAS)

1980 Convention on the Conservation of Antarctic Marine Living Resources (CCAMLR)

1988 Convention on the Regulation of Antarctic Mineral Resource Activities (CRAMRA)

1991 Protocol on Environmental Protection to the Antarctic Treaty (Protocol)

Taken together, as Chapter 6 explores in more detail, they sought to address the leading resource and environmental protection issues confronting the Antarctic, and, in so doing, widened and deepened the institutional architecture of the ATS. Moreover, by building the 'environmental authority' of the ATS, it contributed to the sedimentation of power relations – a select membership of the international community negotiating the present and future states of Antarctica.

Second, for many years, the ATCP did not agree on whether the Antarctic Treaty needed a permanent secretariat, as part of its institutional development. The Antarctic Treaty was, for most of the original participants, intended to be a forum for intergovernmental interaction. In essence, the meetings of the ATCP occurred, initially every two years, and then shifted to every year as the business to be discussed expanded in the 1970s onwards. Each ATCP took it in turn to host a meeting and to organize in effect a temporary secretariat to support the event in question. Other states provided *ad hoc* secretarial support. Argentina, Australia, and Chile, three of the more boisterous claimant states, were widely known to be hostile to the idea of a permanent secretariat during the 1959 negotiations. So a minimalist approach was adopted towards the question of institutional development. The annual meetings were intended to provide a forum for information exchange and discussion of decisions, measures, and recommendations. Topics of interest included jurisdictional questions, scientific cooperation, inspection, and research, alongside the conservation and preservation of Antarctic living resources. Supporting the ATCPs during these meetings, in particular, was the Scientific Committee on Antarctic Research (SCAR), which over the decades has developed a close relationship to the parties in question, providing scientific advice.

Scientific Committee on Antarctic Research (SCAR)

The Scientific (previously Special) Committee on Antarctic Research is a body attached to the International Council for Science. Since February 1958, the UK-based body played a key role in coordinating Antarctic scientific activities, especially in the midst of the International Geophysical Year (1957–8). Ever since its genesis, SCAR has held meetings and has published scientific reports to ensure that scientific knowledge is freely exchanged and monitored by interested parties.

Standing Scientific Groups are a key element of SCAR, and these include the geosciences, life sciences, and physical sciences. One of the newest groups is dedicated to the history of Antarctic science, and thus introduces greater social science and humanities input into the work of SCAR itself.

SCAR provides scientific input and advice to the Antarctic Treaty Consultative Parties.

For further information on SCAR – http://www.scar.org/about/

Even without a permanent secretariat, however, the ATS began to acquire greater institutional strength. The 1972 Seals Convention, for example, provided for the creation of a Commission and Scientific Advisory Committee to help it determine the management of commercial sealing. Likewise, the entry into force of CCAMLR witnessed the creation of a Commission, a Scientific Committee, and a Secretariat based in Hobart. CRAMRA, the mineral regulation regime that never entered into force, envisaged yet further developments including an arbitral tribunal designed to regulate and adjudicate between any parties in dispute. The Protocol on Environmental Protection established a Committee on Environmental Protection, which provides advice on the implementation of the Protocol. Since 1985, the ATCM receives reports from the various commissions and other interested parties including SCAR and the Council of National Antarctic Programmes.

In July 2001, it was decided to establish a Secretariat located in Buenos Aires to assist further in the institutional organization of the ATS. This decision was a long time in coming, given South Africa unsuccessfully proposed such a measure in 1961. The shift in opinion was largely due to an expanded membership (see below) and recognition of the complexity and scope of Antarctic-related activities, especially in the areas of conservation and environmental protection. The sheer volume of business increased accordingly. Formally recognized as desirable in 1985, the 15-year-long period of indecision was shaped by established concerns over the internationalization of the Antarctic, financial costs, functionality, and legal personality, and the location of any secretariat. The UK, for example, was very reluctant to embrace Argentina as a possible location because of concerns that this might encourage further tensions involving the disputed islands of the Falklands/Malvinas and South Georgia, lying outside the Antarctic Treaty's area of application. After a period of Anglo-Argentine rapprochement, the decision to locate the Secretariat in Buenos Aires was eventually secured, and over the last decade has begun taking on the following functions: preparing and supporting ATCM, collecting and publishing the records of the ATCM, facilitating information exchange between parties as required under the Treaty and Protocol, and addressing public enquiries.

Third, the ATS expanded its reach, and the original twelve were joined in the intervening years by a membership encompassing other areas of the world, including other parts of the Americas, Asia, and Europe. In 1959, twelve countries devised a treaty with limited interest from the wider international community with the exception of India. The vast majority of the world's population, especially the colonized world, was not represented at the Washington Conference. In order to be granted full voting rights, new members have to demonstrate 'substantial scientific research' involving not inconsiderable financial investment over an unspecified period. There is no reference in the treaty to how long it might take to be granted consultative party status. In practice, therefore, it depends on the existing membership making that judgement on behalf of others. Between 1961 and 2011, a further 36 countries have acceded to the treaty. There are now 28 consultative parties and 20 non-consultative parties. The latter can attend the ATCP but do not participate in decision-making. They might be able to do so in the future. Notably, in the 1980s, Brazil, China, and India joined the ATS and thus widened the membership, especially from the global South. All three are consultative parties, and thus participate in the business of the ATS. South Africa remains the only African representative. In the 1970s and 1980s, it was a controversial member given its *apartheid* policies, and critics complained that the minority South African governments should not be allowed to continue to participate within the ATS. South African membership acted as a lightening-rod for African critics including Kenya, Zaire, and Nigeria. Using the debating floor of the UN General Assembly, they facilitated debates on the 'question of Antarctica' and highlighted as part of that discussion the illegitimacy of the *apartheid* government. Why, they contended, should an illegitimate government be allowed to participate in a prestigious regional governance system? The ATCP defended South African membership and noted that South Africa was an original member of the Treaty and was not in violation of its provisions.

Finally, the ATS and its membership had to adapt to changing global circumstances including the need to embrace legal and political developments outside the Antarctic – including a gamut of conventions addressing biological diversity, climate change, resource regulation, law of the sea, and commercial activities. This was perhaps the most significant change from those negotiating days of the autumn of 1959. One complicating development was the incorporation of the maritime areas within the Antarctic Treaty area into the remit of the United Nations Law of the Sea Convention (UNCLOS). The Antarctic Treaty, mindful of customary law of the sea, preceded the influential UNCLOS negotiations of the 1970s and 1980s. On the signing of the Third UN Convention in 1982, it was noticeable that the Antarctic was not formally mentioned in the text. But the entry into force of UNCLOS had implications for the Antarctic.

The sovereign rights accruing to coastal states included a 200-nautical-mile exclusive economic zone alongside provisions relating to sovereign rights on the extended continental shelf.

Beyond areas of national jurisdiction, there were areas of common heritage, notably the deep seabed and the high seas. Under Article IV of the Antarctic Treaty, claimant and non-claimant signatories alike agreed to place to one side their disagreements over sovereignty. However, the declaration of maritime zones by claimant states such as Australia has created some interesting tensions. In November 1979, Australia proclaimed a 200-nautical-mile Australian Fishing Zone including the waters of external territories including the Australian Antarctic Territory. This was later revised to exclude the AAT following protests from other parties. Sub-Antarctic island claimants such as Australia, South Africa, and the United Kingdom have been active in defending their sovereign rights north of the Antarctic Treaty area of application. The problem lies within the Antarctic Treaty region and what UNCLOS does to the delicate balance between claimant and non-claimant. In the past, a bi-focal approach to sovereignty had been used to defuse potential tension in that it had been agreed that claimant states could enforce laws involving their national citizens and flagged vessels. All foreign nationals and vessels were exempted in order to preserve the accommodation over sovereignty in the Antarctic.

The burning question raised by UNCLOS is whether coastal states exist in the Antarctic. Are assertions to outer continental shelves in the Antarctic emblematic of either new and/or enlarged claims? Or are they merely extensions of old claims acknowledged under Article 4 of the Antarctic Treaty? Australia and the other claimant states clearly believe that, notwithstanding the provisions of the Antarctic Treaty, they enjoy coastal state rights. One manifestation of this conviction is the submission of materials to the UN Commission on the Limits of the Continental Shelf (CLCS) pertaining to the delineation of the extended coastal shelf (ECS) beyond 200 nautical miles from the coastline. The CLCS, after receipt of relevant geological and geophysical data from coastal states such as Australia, issued a recommendation regarding whether a coastal state has demonstrated the existence of an ECS. The implications of such a move reside in the possible extension of sovereign rights (to exploit submarine resources) across further expanses of the seabed, potentially encompassing thousands of square miles.

Even submitting such materials is controversial, suggesting as it does that claimants like Australia (the first one to submit in November 2004) think they are acting as coastal states within the Antarctic. While the Australian submission encompassed all its offshore territories, it asked the CLCS not to consider the evidence relating to the AAT for the moment. In April 2006, New Zealand excluded a potential outer continental shelf claim from its claimed sector, the Ross Dependency. It reserved the right to dispatch another tranche of materials relating to its Antarctic territories. Argentina in its submission in April 2009 included a map showing an outer continental shelf claim in the contested Antarctic Peninsula. This was the most blatant example of a claimant state believing that it enjoyed coastal state rights in the Antarctic. In May 2009, Norway also submitted materials relating to its Antarctic territory, but asked the CLCS not to consider them for the time being – an example of a partial submission. The UK (May 2008) and France (February 2009) have also opted to make partial submissions, in this case referencing their South Atlantic and South Indian Ocean territories. Chile (May 2009) made what it called a 'preliminary information' statement and noted that a formal submission would be forthcoming.

Due to the unresolved sovereignty-related issues, the CLCS will not formally consider the Antarctic territories, and its recommendations are just that – it is a technical body that is designed to facilitate the delineation and delimitation of the ocean's seabed. The recommendation is based on the CLCS's evaluation of oceanographic and geological data, and the commission members make a judgement on whether they agree with the judgement of coastal states and their mapping of outer continental shelves. It is a complex and expensive business. To

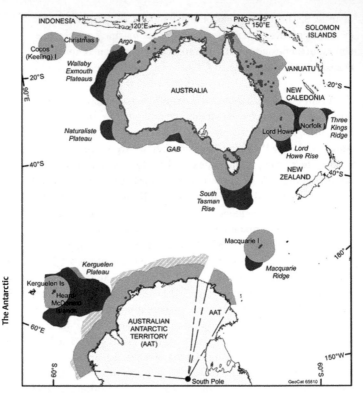

8. Australia's outer continental shelves, including Australian Antarctic territory

generate a submission in the first place depends on substantial investigation of the seabed and careful collation of scientific data. Coastal states are eager to map and agree upon their outer continental shelves because of the extension of sovereign rights to potential resources on the seabed. Unsurprisingly, media commentators have been quick to label this process as akin to a 'scramble for resources', especially if it were to be applied to the disputed Antarctic.

The sovereign rights of coastal states and the common heritage rights of the international community do not sit easily with one another. The submissions produced by coastal states are expensive and time-consuming. The CLCS is a small body and has a huge backlog of submissions to evaluate. It is conservatively estimated that it will take the CLCS some 40–50 years to clear the current waiting list. If, as the United States thinks, there are no coastal states in the Antarctic region, then the waters adjacent to the polar continent would be part of what is termed 'the area'; thus they would be deemed to be part of the common heritage of the international community. Offshore jurisdictional claims in the Antarctic are potentially explosive because they unsettle the existing position of non-recognition of the United States, Russia, and new members such as China and India. It must be noted, however, that the US Senate has yet to ratify UNCLOS despite successive presidents, both Democrat and Republican, urging ratification.

Antarctic accommodations

Over the last 50 years, the Antarctic Treaty and its membership have had to accommodate change and difference. Whatever the appeal of science, and later environmental protection under the terms of the Protocol on Environmental Protection, in terms of cementing solidarity and a unity of shared purpose, the signatories to the treaty have faced their own share of disagreements. While publicly endorsing consensual decision-making, there remains plenty of evidence of disagreement and, at moments, very real tension over the future of the ATS itself. Where there are pressure points, they exist between claimants and non-claimants, consultative parties and third parties, and finally between states and non-state organizations, including non-governmental organizations such as Greenpeace and the Antarctic and Southern Ocean Coalition.

Accommodating the position of the claimant states is a case in point. In 1959, they dominated, numerically at least, the twelve-strong membership. In 2012, the seven claimants are a minority group, albeit an important one. Countries such as Australia, France, New Zealand, and the United Kingdom are active members of the ATS – they contribute substantially to Antarctic science, they advocate policy-making positions, and they contribute to general debates surrounding the Antarctic. They have every incentive to do so. Claimant states remain hugely important in determining the regulation and control of fishing, tourism, and environmental protection. As claimants, north and south of the Antarctic Treaty's area of application, they are prepared to invest in infrastructure and surveillance capabilities, especially when it comes to illegal fishing – that is, fishing that is not regulated or managed by competent authorities.

Fortress Falklands

The 1980s were a tense period for Antarctic Treaty parties as they sought to regulate the possibility of Antarctic mineral resource activity in the future. The negotiations were given added zest because two claimant states – Argentina and Britain – had recently concluded an uneasy settlement following conflict in the Falkland Islands and South Georgia.

After the conflict, the UK government increased funding for British Antarctic Survey (BAS), constructed a new air base at Mount Pleasant in the Falkland Islands, and retained a military presence in South Georgia. Science and the military were instrumental in protecting Britain's South Atlantic empire.

Built in 1985, the base houses between 1,000 and 2,000 British military personnel and varying numbers of aircraft (including the advanced Euro-fighter Typhoon) and helicopters designed for search and rescue. The Falkland Islands community, around 3,000 strong, continues to be a British overseas territory and has enjoyed much improved living conditions thanks to a fishing-licensing regime around the Islands. Oil exploration is ongoing.

The struggle to secure agreement over a minerals regime represented the most significant challenge to the ATS and its ability to maintain consensus. Talk of a possible agreement mobilized opposing parties such as Greenpeace and Malaysia to complain both inside and outside the UN General Assembly that Antarctica was on the verge of being 'carved up' by the wealthy states and their corporations. China and India's membership of the ATS in the early 1980s did little to dispel these fears, especially as it was recognized that the ATS was a secretive organization that held closed meetings. The public rejection of CRAMRA by Australia and France, two claimant states, was a pivotal moment, and led to the speedy negotiation of the Protocol on Environmental Protection in 1991.

Claimant states get rebuffed as well. In 2002, at a meeting of the Commission for the Conservation of Antarctic Marine Living Resources, Australia proposed that the Patagonian Toothfish, a species targeted by illegal, unregulated, and unreported (IUU) fishing around Southern Ocean islands such as the Australian territories of Heard and MacDonald, be placed on Appendix II of the Convention on Trade in Endangered Species of Wild Fauna and Flora (CITES). Notwithstanding support from New Zealand and non-governmental organizations, the proposal was strongly opposed by other members. The Australian proposition was withdrawn, and in the end, another claimant state, Chile, was able to propose that the conservation measures used by CCAMLR to address IUU fishing should prevail. The hostility towards CITES can be explained with reference to the fact that some members of the ATS fear growing encroachment into the Antarctic by global legal instruments to the point where the authority of the ATS might be compromised in the longer term.

Non-claimants such as the United States, the Soviet Union/ Russia, and, more recently, China and India increasingly matter. Take China as an example. Initially eager to exclude China from the Antarctic programme of the IGY, the United States and others have had to recognize China's expanding presence in the Antarctic. Starting in the 1970s, Chinese parties contacted Australian and New Zealand experts for advice on creating an Antarctic scientific programme. In 1981, the Chinese National Antarctic Expedition Committee was established, and China joined the ATS in 1983. Within two years, the country was a consultative party (compared to other signatories who have had to wait for many years to be confirmed as an ATCP) and established its first base at King George Island in the South Shetlands. Over the next decade, with fluctuating funds and political priorities, new research stations were built and collaborations extended to include European, North American, and Asian countries, including the UK and US. Using the precedents established by the earlier parties to the Antarctic Treaty, science and scientific research provided a mechanism for extending the Chinese presence within and beyond the Antarctic. In 2005, a team of Chinese polar explorers travelled to Dome Argus (A), one of the least explored areas of the Antarctic.

The Antarctic map is now encumbered with a new set of place names recording this achievement – Turtle Mountain, Snake Mountain, and Western Lake – reflecting Chinese history and geography. As a consequence, Western journalists frequently represent China's 'rise' in the Antarctic (and the Arctic) as a worrying development, mirroring earlier preoccupation with the Soviet Union and its polar programme in the 1950s. Chinese scientists and political leaders, as with earlier members, understand well the logics and techniques associated with the ATS. Scientific and exploratory achievement, combined with networking and collaboration, are the key mechanisms for achieving influence within this organization. The Chinese government was eager to secure the support of the ATS for its plans to build a scientific station at Dome A (established in 2009), while at the same time clashing with Australia over criticism of illegal fishing in the Southern Ocean. Compared to other members, however, its scientific output remains modest, and further development will depend on resource commitments in the future.

China and India's membership of the ATS remind us that two large Asian states are increasingly making their presence felt in the Antarctic. In October 2010, India announced its inaugural scientific expedition to the South Pole, and the news was well received within the country as evidence of its 'rise' in world affairs. Involved in the Antarctic since 1981, India first raised the status of the polar continent in the United Nations in the 1950s. With several research stations established, India has been a very public advocate of the Antarctic being a common heritage of mankind. In 2007, at the India-hosted annual consultative party meeting, the then External Affairs Minister, Pranab Mukherjee, reaffirmed that 'Antarctica being a common heritage of mankind, and the foremost symbol of peaceful use and cooperation needs to be protected for posterity'. As with China, India's presence in the ATS is another reminder that there is a group of 'global states' that have not only rejected the rights of the seven claimant states but also articulated a view of the Antarctic which is fundamentally different to the view of the United States. A common heritage of mankind, building upon UN General Assembly resolutions and international legal precedent, suggests that the Antarctic should be held in trust for future generations and not be subject to exploitation by individual states.

Finally, it is worth noting that non-state organizations are accommodated within the political architecture of the ATS. This was not always so. In 1959, twelve states and their representatives were at the negotiating table in Washington, DC. At the latest Consultative Meeting, held in Buenos Aires in June–July 2011, delegations were mingling with environmental groups, journalists, multi-national corporations, tour operators, academics, and policy-orientated consultants, and professional groupings such as the Council of Managers of National Antarctic Programs (CONAP). It is not uncommon for representatives from environmental movements to accompany national delegations. Compared to the first Consultative Meeting held in Australia in 1961, the business of the ATS is a lot more accessible to non-consultative parties, even if there is still much business conducted away from the direct gaze of interested parties. The Antarctic Secretariat, moreover, provides a great deal more information about the business conducted at the annual meetings, alongside other activities such as the Committee on Environmental Protection, which is charged with implementing and reviewing the Protocol on Environmental Protection.

The enduring treaty

As a governance regime, the Antarctic Treaty is frequently been trumpeted as a success story. Why has it endured? I think there are three fundamental reasons, apart from all the original parties getting something tangible from the 1959 negotiations. First, the twelve parties produced an attractive creation myth: they used science and scientists to portray themselves as political visionaries seeking to introduce peace and harmony to a remote continent. While the experiences of the IGY and science in general were important, this was an emollient for a treaty created out of claims and counter-claims. The treaty could not settle the disputed ownership issue because it was not solvable. But to the excluded wider world, it was important to 'sell' the Antarctic Treaty as progressive and attuned to the principles embodied in the United Nations Charter.

Second, the treaty endured because there were provisions (and opportunities taken) to not only accommodate new members but also to deal with issues such as conservation, environmental protection, and living resource exploitation as they arose. The treaty, with its associated conventions and protocols, proved flexible. Even at moments of greatest political tension, such as over the prospect of potential mineral exploitation in the 1980s, the Antarctic Treaty parties proved sufficiently adept at neutralizing opposition as voiced in the United Nations General Assembly. They did so by inviting some of the most powerful critics such as India and China to join the treaty and by signing a Protocol on Environmental Protection, which banned all forms of mining in the Antarctic Treaty region (defined as south of 60°S latitude). The earliest any review conference can be called is 2048.

Third, the treaty endured because the provisions of Article IV were sufficiently vague to allow competing positions to co-exist, however uneasily. Article IV dealt with the potentially explosive issue of sovereignty claims. Getting agreement on this issue was helped, paradoxically perhaps, by the occurrence of the Cold War. It was clear that the Soviet Union and the United States did not want to make the Antarctic another area of strain given prevailing tensions over the Arctic Ocean. It also helped that no one was contemplating mining and resource extraction in the late 1950s. If anything, parties were more concerned about the frozen continent becoming a nuclear testing ground. So Article IV suited all concerned and, as noted earlier, there were only twelve parties to negotiate with. Compare such a situation to contemporary climate change summits and conferences where it is common to deal with over a hundred governments and political leaders and, something that did not exist in the 1950s, 24/7 news reporting cycles and attending pressures to be seen to 'doing something'. The Antarctic is far more demanding of our attention.

Summary

The governance of the Antarctic has changed markedly even during the lifetime of the Antarctic Treaty. The international peace and stability established by the Antarctic Treaty remains essential in ensuring the continued participation by major non-claimants such as China, India, Russia, and the United States. The potential for discord and possible conflict in the future exists. Resources have always haunted human activity in the Antarctic. The sovereignty of the region is unresolved, and the attitude of the United States in particular will remain pivotal to the longer-term health of the ATS as an international regime of governance.

China and India will, over time, increasingly make their presence felt on and off the ice. As the Chinese Ambassador, Yin Hengmin, reminded his audience at the Commemorative Meeting of the 50th Anniversary of the entry into force of the Antarctic Treaty:

> Most of the Antarctic issues are of global nature. No single state could address them alone. All relevant states should put joint effort to stress the fundamental role of scientific research and to improve the co-operation amongst scientists and to strengthen the interaction between scientists and policy makers. Co-operation should be enhanced within the frameworks of the Antarctic Treaty System, the United Nations Convention of the Law of the Sea, and international maritime conventions etc. Political wisdom should be exerted and necessary compromise should be made for common interests. China will continue, as always, to work together with scientists and policy makers from all over the world, and contribute to the peace, stability and sustainable development of the Antarctic region.

Notwithstanding such a sonorous declaration, China and the United States, if they were truly serious about promoting the 'sustainable development of the Antarctic region', might consider not only ongoing issues such as fishing and bio-prospecting, but also global climatic disruption of the Antarctic itself. Perhaps the greatest governance challenge facing the Antarctic, therefore, is not to be found anywhere in the region. At one time, men wrote harrowing accounts of their encounters with the ice; now, humans worry about saving the ice from further melting.

Chapter 5
Doing Antarctic science

The Antarctic has often been described as a space for science and a space of science. As the Swedish historian of science Aant Elzinga put it, 'the construction of a continent by and for science'. Since the 18th-century voyages of Captain Cook, exploration and science (and the two continue to go hand in hand) have played a critical role in helping to construct 'the Antarctic' in terms of Western expectations and understandings – as a place that needed to be both 'uncovered' and 'incorporated' into an expanding pool of planetary knowledge. Since the 1940s and 1950s, the widespread notion that the Antarctic functions as a 'scientific laboratory' at the proverbial end of the world, with due emphasis given to controlled and ordered knowledge creation and international behaviour, remains a powerful framing device. Paradoxically, it has helped to legitimate and justify billions of dollars, pounds, francs, and other currencies of investment, while providing a *modus operandi* for the continued colonization and occupation of the Antarctic. Claimant and non-claimant states alike continue to cite and site science as the principal reason for their involvement in the southern polar region, even if it is perfectly possible to infer other interests such as resource, strategic, and territorial factors.

With the entry into force of the Antarctic Treaty in June 1961, in the aftermath of the International Geophysical Year 1957–8, this dominant framing was reinforced in successive meetings of the Antarctic Treaty Consultative Parties (ATCPs). Science, in combination with ideals of collaboration and free information exchange, provided (and continues to provide) an attractive vision of and for a place characterized by the absence of conflict and discord. Who could object to a continent dedicated to science in the midst of Cold War antagonism? Ideologically, this idea of science as driving Antarctic activities was useful for several inter-related reasons – it helped to bind the signatories together with a common sense of purpose; it encouraged others to assume that intellectual enquiry was paramount rather than territorial/resource/strategic intrigue; and finally, it provided a mechanism for controlling the entry into the Antarctic Treaty System of other parties, and a means for disciplining existing parties.

The role of science was multi-faceted, never more so than in the Cold War period – and never politically innocent. During the Antarctic Treaty period (and before it), science became a new and subtle form of geopolitics, and had at least four potential roles. Science was a vehicle for leadership and prestige. Claimants and non-claimants used their scientific projects and infrastructural development to project power inside and outside the Antarctic. Science continued to offer collaborative possibilities, and Cold War adversaries (including the two superpowers) exchanged scientists and organized research station placements. Science provided a form of regime security for the ATS, enabling countries to continue to demilitarize the region. As long as all the participants conducted scientific activities, and respected the provisions of the Antarctic Treaty, there was no apparent need to undermine the prohibition on military activities. Finally, science provided a useful foil to those would-be critics, including members of the developing world, worried about improper uses of the Antarctic. This was particularly sensitive in the 1970s and 1980s. While Antarctic geologists might indirectly be investigating and evaluating the resource potential of the region, to the wider world, it appeared that they were seeking to better understand the geological history of the polar continent and surrounding ocean.

The Janus-faced nature of Antarctic science sits uneasily with the claims that are made routinely about the Antarctic as a site of and node for global environmental debates. In December 2009, the Scientific Committee on Antarctic Research (SCAR) released a report entitled 'Antarctic Climate Change and the Environment', which brought the significance of the Antarctic to the attention of policy-makers. As Colin Summerhayes, Executive Director of SCAR, noted:

> Antarctica is an unrivalled source of information about our planet... by integrating this multidisciplinary evidence into a single source we will help scientists and policy makers understand the distinction between environmental changes linked to Earth's natural cycles, and those that are human induced.

However, it is also the case that the seven claimant states, including two Antarctic science leaders, Australia and Britain, tend to operate scientific stations in their sectors, and concentrate funding overwhelmingly in research-related projects therein. Meanwhile, others such as Argentina are remarkably explicit about the role that science plays in consolidating 'their' sovereignty in the Argentine Antarctic Territory, notwithstanding Article IV of the Antarctic Treaty. In the Argentine scientific, technical, and services plan (2010), readers are reminded that a key objective of Antarctic-related activity is:

> to consolidate Argentine sovereignty rights in the Antarctic, going deeper in the scientific and technical activities aiming at attaining full knowledge of the Antarctic nature, specifically the areas related to the country's priorities, promoting conservation and preservation of fishing and mineral resources, environmental protection, Latin-American integration in Antarctic matters and rendering of services.

Science does geopolitical work, and this is true of both past and present. Argentina is not unique in this regard, but simply best seen as one of the most emphatic. The science of whaling, as the next chapter suggests, was an essential element in the armoury of imperial Britain. Science not only informed policy-making but provided a form of 'environmental authority' enabling territorial control. Scientific interest in the relationship between climate change and ice sheets provided the public justification for the multi-national NSBX in the early 1950s even if there was a covert territorial rationale.

Science and the 1959 Antarctic Treaty

The Antarctic Treaty notes that the Antarctic is a place in which scientific investigation should prevail. The preamble to the treaty is explicit in this regard – science is linked to the progress of mankind more generally. As the preamble notes:

> *Convinced* that the establishment of a firm foundation for the continuation and development of such cooperation on the basis of freedom of scientific investigation in Antarctica as applied during the International Geophysical Year accords with the interests of science and the progress of all mankind.

The highlighting of the word 'convinced' is indicative of the general conceit of the treaty and its genesis. Article II of the Treaty enshrines the principle of freedom of scientific research, and Article III promotes the free exchange of scientific information and research personnel, with due emphasis given to transparency and openness with regard to expeditionary movement in and out of the Antarctic. Article VII established a system of inspection in relation to all scientific stations, aircraft, and ships operating in the polar region. Science was considered to be the mechanism par excellence for confidence-building and the reinforcement of norms among the original signatories to the Antarctic Treaty.

Science and scientific operations remains prioritized, as Secretary Clinton might note, within the Antarctic Treaty System, even if the range of interested parties has widened in the intervening period (1961–2011). With the entry into force of the 1991 Protocol on Environmental Protection, for example, scientific-related activity is exempted from the strict rules concerning interference with Antarctic wildlife and access to areas judged to be ecologically vulnerable. For new members seeking to join the ATS, it is Antarctic science rather than participation within Antarctic fishing and/or tourism that determines whether, under the terms of Article XI of the Antarctic Treaty, a country might be admitted into the membership. In a deliberate attempt to limit the potential membership, countries aspiring to consultative party status needed to show evidence of 'substantial scientific activity'. In the 1990s, after criticism about the replication of research stations and over-concentration of scientific activity in the more accessible Antarctic Peninsula region, the demand was relaxed that aspiring consultative parties establish a permanent research station as set out in Article IX (2):

> Each Contracting Party which has become a party to the present Treaty by accession under Article XIII shall be entitled to appoint representatives to participate in the meetings referred to in paragraph 1 of the present Article, during such times as that Contracting Party demonstrates its interest in Antarctica by conducting substantial research activity there, such as the establishment of a scientific station or the dispatch of a scientific expedition.

Consultative parties such as the Netherlands have never established a permanent research station in the Antarctic, for example.

Antarctic science is a form of symbolic capital within the ATS, with value in subtle and not so subtle forms. In the 1980s, for example, it was not uncommon to read criticism of some national Antarctic programmes for their poor scientific productivity and staffing levels of research stations, with particular ire aimed at Argentina and Chile due to their over-representation of military personnel. When British scientists and administrators made such criticism, in the aftermath of the 1982 Falklands/Malvinas War, it is not difficult to see how this critique might be seen as geopolitically self-serving. Given the persistence of overlapping claims in the Antarctic Peninsula region, it suited British interests to highlight the gulf in scientific productivity and to note that the UK, along with the US, Germany, and Australia, were some of the most productive consultative parties in the ATS in terms of peer-reviewed Antarctic science. The quality of British science has long been used as a marker of its validity compared to the quantity provided by others, including allies – British polar administrator Brian Roberts complained in the early 1950s that American expeditions such as High Jump were not a patch on the 'useful' and 'unostentatious' work by the modestly funded Falkland Islands Dependencies Survey. Such scientific credentials contribute greatly to wider influence within the ATS and play a part in consolidating the scientific budgets of operators such as British Antarctic Survey, which received a funding boost post-Falklands conflict.

Science as a tool of national strategy remains undisturbed by the provisions of the Antarctic Treaty and associated legal instruments, notwithstanding demands for international collaboration, inspection, and information exchange. All seven of the claimant states maintain permanent research stations in their sectors, and geographically concentrate scientific activity. They are able to do so in part because others contribute knowledge and understanding in other areas of the Antarctic – even if concerns have been raised about why so many research stations are located in the Antarctic Peninsula region compared to the polar interior.

Globalizing Antarctic science

The first IPY of 1882–3 established a platform for the subsequent three incarnations, in that it was collaborative and interdisciplinary in nature and committed to advancing scientific knowledge about the polar regions. While the Arctic region dominated the first two polar years of 1882–3 and 1932–3, the third and fourth (1957–8 International Geophysical year and 2007–9 respectively) witnessed a greater profile for both the Antarctic and bi-polar research investigation. Compared to the 19th century, new technologies including satellites, autonomous machinery, and novel techniques such as DNA profiling have revolutionized the conduct and scope of Antarctic science.

Akin to a scientific Olympics, the 1957–8 IGY was one of the most ambitious global programmes of research involving 60,000 scientists and some 67 countries; 48 Antarctic bases were operational during 18 months of intense scientific research, and some disciplines such as geology were deliberately excluded so that the spectre of resource potential did not derail the collaborative ethos of IGY. A special committee for the IGY (later renamed Scientific Committee of Antarctic Research, SCAR) was charged with coordinating national programmes, and the twelve participating members agreed where countries would establish their research stations in order to fill 'gaps' in coverage of the polar continent in particular. This led to major exploratory research not only on the surface of the Antarctic but, significantly, upwards into the atmosphere and beyond. Horizontal and vertical forms of exploration were combined in a far more systematic and extensive way than before. Research into the ionosphere and aurora were complemented by studies examining the thickness of the ice sheet and topographical mapping. One of the most spectacular achievements were the seismic soundings of the Antarctic ice sheet by American teams led by Charles Bentley. By the end of the IGY, most of the Antarctic had been seen, at least from the air, and the physical characteristics of the region mapped and measured. Extraordinary as this achievement might have been, the IGY will

9. Logo of the International Geophysical Year (IGY)

for the most part always be remembered for the launch of the Soviet satellite *Sputnik*.

The legacy of the IGY, apart from generating vast quantities of information about the Antarctic and outer space, was to outline the possibilities for the globalization of polar science. Newly created organizations such as SCAR provided a practical mechanism for coordinating scientific endeavours, at the same time as early negotiations unfolded regarding a possible Antarctic Treaty. Intellectually, the IGY signalled a shift away from using knowledge created elsewhere to understand the Antarctic to using the Antarctic to understand other regions, including outer space. In that sense, the official logo of the IGY was well selected – a tilted globe with the Antarctic/South Pole prioritized alongside an orbiting satellite travelling high above the Earth's surface. The IGY logo also portrays a globe without any political markings and nation states, a reminder again that geopolitical divisions had no place in the conduct of the earth sciences and the generation of global scientific knowledge.

The fourth IPY, running between March 2007 and March 2009, in order to allow two field seasons, was the most ambitious ever, and included unprecedented opportunities for public involvement, especially in the inhabited Arctic. Involving 50,000 people – including 10,000 scientists and associated logistical support staff and 60 countries– the fourth IPY supported some 200 Arctic and Antarctic projects. As with the IGY some 50 years earlier, the rationale for those approved projects lay in a widely held belief that the polar regions are experiencing significant environmental changes and that there remains a pressing need to better understand the physical and biological dynamics of the Antarctic and Arctic. Leaving a legacy of new and or enhanced observation systems, facilities, and infrastructure was considered to be critical by the IPY planning group, because long-term data collection and analysis is essential for making sense of the current and future transformation of the Antarctic and its connections to the rest of the planet. In contrast to the IGY logo, the fourth IPY emphasized the role of people, both in the generation and engagement of polar knowledge, and the arrow encapsulating the globe no longer evokes the *Sputnik* trajectory. Unlike the IGY logo, English is the only language represented, indicative of the fact that so much polar science is presented and written in English.

The IPY demonstrates only too clearly the hegemonic position of science within the Antarctic. The explicit rationale of IPY was to collect and process information on the polar regions specifically and connect up with global processes affecting the Earth generally. Antarctic science has also revealed some counter-intuitive and cautionary findings. The well-publicized discovery of the ozone hole in the 1980s by British Antarctic Survey scientists led to widespread global concern about atmospheric/stratospheric change and the likely implications of increased UV-B radiation for human and non-human communities. But that loss of ozone has also protected the Antarctic from global warming, especially outside the Antarctic Peninsula region. The loss of ozone has intensified the polar vortex and led to no significant temperature changes in the polar interior and increased sea ice extent in the Southern Ocean. As Professor John Turner of British Antarctic Survey noted:

For me the most astonishing evidence is the way one man-made environmental impact – the ozone hole – has shielded most of Antarctica from another – global warming. Understanding the complexities surrounding these issues is a challenge for scientists–and communicating these in a meaningful way to society and to policymakers is essential.

Telling stories: Pine Island Glacier

Pine Island Glacier in West Antarctica has provided important clues as to the nature of Antarctic warming. It is a huge geographical feature and discharges some 100 trillion tons of ice into the Amundsen Sea every year. Monitored by satellites and airborne surveying for the last 30 years, this glacier attracted scientific interest because it was grounded below sea level and was vulnerable to potential change because it lacked any protection from a floating extension of ice.

Since the early 1990s, scientists have noted that the glacier is retreating inland, and is increasingly exposed to erosive Antarctic waters. This exposure to warmer waters, by the standards of the Antarctic, is contributing significantly to ice mass loss. The fate of this glacier is, as a consequence, widely regarded as emblematic of the future stability of the Antarctic ice sheet, and possible sea level rise in the future.

Recent and ongoing scientific projects in the Antarctic

Antarctic science is, by its very nature, multi-disciplinary and collaborative, often involving multiple countries and organizations. SCAR, as noted above, plays an important role in coordinating and organizing. The examples discussed below are intended to give a sense of where some of this research endeavour is heading. In general terms, Antarctic science is not only focused on better understanding the Antarctic and Southern Ocean, but also and increasingly addressing the connections between the region and the rest of planet Earth. In scientific terms, the Antarctic is no longer considered a 'pole apart' and now attracts ever more interest from those who may not have considered themselves polar scientists *per se*.

1. Antarctic Gamburtsev Mountain Project

The Gamburtsev mountain range, dubbed Antarctica's 'ghost mountains' by the British Antarctic Survey, is a sub-glacial feature located in East Antarctica close to Dome A. Discovered in 1958 by a Soviet Antarctic Expedition, the range itself was named after the geophysicist Grigoriy Gamburtsev. The mountain range is about 750 miles long, with an altitude of about 8,000–9,000 feet, and is covered by approximately 2,000 feet of ice and snow. Until quite recently, there was limited understanding of how this geographical feature, similar in nature to the European Alps, was created. This mountain range matters because scientists believe that it will provide important clues not only as to how the East Antarctic ice sheet developed, but also to future changes as a consequence of global warming trends.

As part of the IPY, a multi-national team investigated the geological history of the mountain range. One of the key findings is that the ice sheets covering the mountains are growing at the base, whereby widespread re-freezing contributes to the consolidation of the base of the ice sheet. As one of the scientists, Robin Bell of Columbia University, remarked:

> Water has always been known to be important to ice sheet dynamics, but mostly as a lubricant. As ice sheets change, we want to predict how they will change. Our results show that models [attempting to understand the future trajectory of ice-sheet stability] must include water [and its potential role] beneath.

Sub-glacial water, far from being marginal, holds the key to better understanding ice-sheet dynamics, especially when then linked to debates about the impact of global warming on the Antarctic and future sea level change.

The freezing and re-freezing of sub-glacial water not only contributes to ice-sheet dynamics and their modelling but also initially confused researchers who were puzzled by the existence of a series of re-frozen structures underneath the ice sheet – no one believed that water moving underneath a great mass of ice sheet could fundamentally alter its structure. As water was being melted and re-frozen, under the ice sheet, it was being transported uphill towards mountain ridges where the ice sheet was thinner. On re-freezing, new structures were being fashioned at the base of the ice sheet – creating what were termed 'ghostly mountains'. Consequently, older ice is pushed to the surface of the ice sheet, thus making it more accessible for scientists to access evidence of past climates.

The role of re-freezing will continue to be a major area of future research in both the Antarctic and Greenland ice sheets. The distribution of water under the ice sheet is now understood to be absolutely critical to understanding ice-sheet dynamics and whether it will be easier to predict future decay or not. This was not the case even a decade ago.

2. Million Year Plus Ice Core Project (MY+)

While the 'Million Year Plus Ice Core Project' sounds like a marketing gimmick, it actually highlights something rather important about what we understand about the earth's oldest ice. It is emblematic of the work of the International Partnerships in Ice Core Sciences (IPICS), which is a group of scientists from over 20 countries with an active interest in the topic. Four priority projects, including this one, have been identified, with the aim of trying to retrieve ice over 1–1.5 million years old from the East Antarctic plateau in particular.

With the help of existing ice core data, scientists have been able to ruminate about 'ice ages' occurring every 100,000 years or so. Before then, 'ice age' frequency was around 40,000 years. Thus, the aim of the MY+ Ice Core Project is to help scientists to better understand dramatic shifts in the frequency of ice ages, and the role that gases such as carbon dioxide play in climate change. As Eric Wolf, a senior scientist at British Antarctic Survey, explained to me, the rationale for going beyond 800,000 years is a profound one. If patterns of climate variability changed (e.g. 100,000- and 40,000-year cycles involving cold glacial and warm interglacial periods), then we need to better understand why this underlying natural pattern, well before human industrialization and urbanization, occurred. It is believed that the presence of carbon dioxide is crucial in shaping ice transition.

Thus, the extraction of ice cores has revolutionized scientific debates on climate change, because the analysis of trapped atmospheric bubbles contributes to better understanding why the Earth's climate has shifted. These trapped bubbles help reveal what greenhouse gases such as carbon dioxide were like hundreds of thousands of years ago. Ice core research has already confirmed that we are currently experiencing a comparatively mild interglacial phase within a series of warm/cold oscillations. Scientists are eager to better understand what causes these natural climatic cycles, so that we understand what caused the length of these cycles to alter by some 60,000 years, and possibly relate this shift to a lowering of atmospheric carbon dioxide concentrations.

Led by the Australian Antarctic Division, the MY+ project will extract a complete ice core from an area of the Antarctic in which the ice is thickest. Within the Australian Antarctic Territory, the Aurora Basin close to the Australian scientific station of Casey was identified as suitable because ice cover is over 2 miles in depth with a low snow accumulation rate and low ice velocity. The project itself, launched as part of a contribution to the IPY, will take something like five summer seasons of drilling and another three to four years of ice core analysis. Such a deep ice core, with embedded evidence of past gaseous concentrations, will be essential in order to reconstruct climate history some one million plus years ago and complements research on sub-glacial lakes with a focus on the pre-glacial history of the Antarctic. For a claimant state such as Australia, support for the project from the 18 other members of the International Partnerships in Ice Core Sciences group is important, and unquestionably useful in cementing Australian leadership in Antarctic science, and it is worth remembering that there has been much media and policy-related debate in the country about the need to maintain investment in science and infrastructure in the massive Australian Antarctic Territory. This project reminds us again that science and geopolitics work closely with one another even if they appear to be separate.

3. Census of Antarctic Marine Life (CAML)

Following the 2007–9 International Polar Year, a Census of Antarctic Marine Life (CAML) revealed that over 235 marine organisms are found in both the Arctic Ocean and Southern Ocean. Larger creatures such as whales and birds undertake this bi-polar migration on an annual basis, and smaller creatures such as sea cucumbers and snails are common to both polar oceans. Marine currents and fairly uniform temperatures in the deep ocean are believed to be the key drivers of this extraordinary movement of species. For the Antarctic itself, the CAML noted 9,350 verified species, ranging in size from the microbe to the Blue Whale.

Thus, the CAML investigated Antarctic marine biodiversity, and considered how climate change has affected the abundance and distribution of marine life in the Southern Ocean. This project, operating between 2005 and 2010, aimed to enhance public and scientific understanding, in the light of fears that ongoing climate change is disrupting marine biota uniquely adapted to extreme environments. Seventeen research vessels during IPY were traversing the Southern Ocean, collecting samples, mapping species records, and cataloguing specimens. The idea of the census is to provide a benchmark for future studies on the extraordinary range of creatures inhabiting the Antarctic's cold waters. While documenting different species matters, one major outcome has been to locate marine biodiversity 'hotspots'.

One such hotspot is the Ross Sea. Accounting for only 2% of the Southern Ocean, the Ross Sea is an embayment between East and West Antarctica. Its claim to marine biodiversity fame lies in the strong presence of top predators in the Southern Ocean food chain. According to scientists, nearly 40% of the world's Adélie Penguins are to be found in the Ross Sea, along with 25% of Emperor Penguins and thousands of whales, seals, and large finfish including the commercially lucrative Patagonian Toothfish – a favoured target of the Ross Sea Killer Whale. This high density of so-called top predators is very unusual in marine environments in terms of dominating the system's biomass and driving the entire ecosystem. The current norm, in terms of the ecological pyramid, is the predominance of phytoplankton at the base, with small numbers of top predators at the apex of the pyramid.

One area of research, as a consequence of this unusual ecological profile, is to imagine the Ross Sea region as not unusual in one sense but merely indicative of an environment where commercial fishing has not (yet) decimated top predators such as fish, seals, and whales. Typically, the predatory life in the Ross Sea consume zooplankton, usually krill and copepods. By the end of the summer season, levels of zooplankton have declined and the larger predators such as whales and penguins turn to eating smaller predators such as silverfish, and the end result is that there remains a large amount of phytoplankton, which is not consumed by the now depleted krill. Sinking to the ocean floor, the phytoplankton help to nourish the benthic floor (the lowest level of water in an ocean or lake), and thus generate a biodiversity hotspot for hundreds of species of invertebrates such as sponges and corals.

The CAML revealed that the Ross Sea was one of the world's least disrupted marine ecosystems. The impact of human behaviour was low compared to many other environments, even within the Antarctic itself. But this will change, not least because New Zealand in particular decided to license commercial fishing for Patagonian Toothfish in 1996, and this has led to increased extraction of the species by a host of trawler fleets registered to New Zealand, Argentina, Spain, Korea, and Russia. While the Convention for the Conservation of Antarctic Marine Living Resources (CCAMLR) places emphasis on the sustainable exploitation of Southern Ocean fisheries, scientists fear that the commercial fishing industry will have a dramatic impact on the Patagonian Toothfish population and wider implications for the ecological pyramid of the Ross Sea.

Future challenges for this ongoing research into the Southern Ocean include further identification of species, many of which remain to be discovered by marine biologists. Hard-to-reach areas such as under floating ice shelves, the deep sea, and so-called novel environments such as hydrothermal vents, methane seeps, and seamounts serve as a timely reminder that Southern Ocean science co-exists with ongoing exploration. While the CAML revealed the richness of these ecosystems, only about half of the Antarctic shelf fauna, much less a fraction of deep-sea animals, have been identified. Some estimates suggest that it could take decades to carry out species identification, including the discovery of new isopods, including crabs and shrimps inhabiting the Southern Ocean.

In the early part of the 21st century, the CAML reminds us that science has not eclipsed exploration. We are still continuing to map and survey the Antarctic, and this mosaic of environments continues to surprise and delight scientists. There continue to be new spaces of polar exploration.

4. The Lake Ellsworth Consortium

Sub-glacial lakes, including Lake Vostok, have attracted a great deal of scientific interest, and over 150 lakes have been discovered under the Antarctic ice sheet. In Lake Vostok's case, we have a feature equivalent in size to Lake Ontario – some 7,500 square miles – and made possible by geothermal heating from the interior of the Earth. Using radio-echo sounding, these lakes generate curiosity precisely because they have been isolated for a considerable period of time, and as a consequence of their isolation possess unique biological habitats. These environments are, by virtue of their subterranean location, profoundly influenced by the absence of sunlight, very low nutrient levels, and extraordinary pressures due to the weight of the overlaying ice. For interested scientists, these sub-glacial lakes are not only fascinating in their own right in terms of understanding the Antarctic's evolutionary history, but also potentially important for better understanding the subterranean environments of other planets and satellites, such as Jupiter's moon Europa, which possesses an icy crust above a liquid water mass.

The ongoing exploration of Lake Ellsworth in West Antarctica is a good example of how research in this area of the Antarctic must contend with the most challenging of constraints, such as the avoidance of contaminating the lake in question. Lake Ellsworth is over 100 metres deep, and this sub-glacial lake is regarded as scientifically promising. In order to better understand the local environment of Lake Ellsworth, 30 scientists led by the University of Edinburgh and British Antarctic Survey will have to drill, sample, and study this unique and uncontaminated environment.

During the IPY, the multi-institutional team, using radar and seismic surveys, were able to map and measure the lake's outline and water depth. Ice-penetrating radar is essential because radio waves help to identify sub-glacial lakes, as opposed to ice and rock. As a consequence of the flat and uniformly strong echo, it is comparatively straightforward to discover the sub-glacial lakes *per se*. Sediment coring will follow in order to better understand the ice sheet history of West Antarctica. For 2012/3, funding has been secured so that the Lake Ellsworth team can begin to drill into the overlying ice sheet and to the lake water itself. A probe and sediment corer would follow to test for biotic life and secure sediment from the lake floor respectively. In November 2012, the team hope to drill using hot water. Once they reach their target depth of 3,000 metres, having established a hole of about 36 centimetres in diameter, they will have 24 hours to collect water samples and sediment cores before re-freezing sets in.

The wider significance of the Lake Ellsworth project lies in its contribution to better understanding, as with research on the Gamburtsev Mountains, the counter-intuitive importance of liquid water to the polar continent – extraordinary low temperatures and substantial ice sheet notwithstanding. The Antarctic ice sheet is effectively warmed by geothermal heating and, as a consequence, water flows into troughs and valleys where it forms a patchwork of sub-glacial lakes, some extending thousands of square miles in area. Sediments from sub-glacial lakes may, it is hoped, enhance understanding of ice-sheet stability and, in the worst-case scenario, ice-sheet collapse.

Summary

Science is still the number one activity in the Antarctic in terms of both scale – most practised – and morality – most legitimate. Scientists have, collectively and collaboratively, with the help of bodies such as SCAR, generated some extraordinarily important insights into the Antarctic. It is a critical part of planet Earth. The physical and biological characteristics of the polar continent and Southern Ocean are closely related to other areas of the global environmental system. One of the greatest achievements of the International Polar Years has been to demonstrate and highlight to both professional and public audiences that the polar regions are neither remote nor isolated. Ocean and atmosphere exchange, migratory movement, and the circulation of human activity all contribute, in their varied ways, to a profound sense of interconnection. The Antarctic also holds some of the richest archival evidence of past climate change and biological indicators of the contemporary and possibly future environments. With 90% of the world's ice and 70% of the world's fresh water, the Antarctic is central to all our fates.

One cautionary note that Antarctic science continues to contribute is geographical in nature. While we might note warming trends, it is striking that there are always regional and local variations to factor into any assessment of Antarctic climate change and environmental debates. In the case of meteorological research, for example, the Antarctic Peninsula region has witnessed both increased snowfall at the same time as scientists have noted warming trends, especially in the summer season, on the eastern portion of the Peninsula. The waters of the Southern Ocean are experiencing warming, as a consequence of increasing westerly winds interfering with the capacity of the water to absorb carbon dioxide, and the sea ice extent in the winter season has increased, especially in the Ross Sea region. The Antarctic Peninsula, however, has experienced a decrease in sea ice extent because of those aforementioned warming trends. All of this means that Antarctic scientists face the daunting task of making sense of an immensely complex series of terrestrial and marine environments intimately connected to regional and global climate and oceanic systems.

If we can say anything about the future in the Antarctic, it is most likely to involve the following combination – decreased sea ice extent, loss of ice from the West Antarctic ice sheet, retreating glaciers, and changing ecosystem dynamics as a consequence of ocean acidification and global warming. Climate data, both from manned and automatic research stations such as Halley, Dome C, and Rothera, continue to provide vital information about monthly mean temperatures and pressure readings. By 2100, some scientific models are predicting that sea level will rise by up to 1.5 metres, and as the Antarctic warms, so new plant and animal communities will begin to transform life in a melting freezer.

Chapter 6
Exploiting and protecting the Antarctic

For all the 14 Articles of the Antarctic Treaty, comparatively little attention was given to resource management and environmental protection of the Antarctic. At only about 2,300 words long, it remains a remarkably brief legal document, which, as noted earlier, provided a sufficiently flexible and resilient framework for future legal and political development. Human impact on the Antarctic's terrestrial and marine ecosystems derives principally from the exploitation of living natural resources such as seals, whales, fish, and krill. While the Protocol on Environmental Protection, an additional legal instrument to the Antarctic Treaty (signed in 1991, entered into force 1998), prohibits all forms of mineral exploitation, the Antarctic bears witness to the capacity of humanity to exploit massively non-human populations in ways that have proved anything but sustainable.

Resources have been extracted from the Antarctic since the 18th century. While there were explorers eager to inquire, there were commercial operators eager to acquire. And, of course, some were perfectly capable of doing both. As with the Arctic, exploitation began with sealing, whaling, and fishing, culminating with biological prospecting involving Antarctic living matter. During the sealing period, from the 1780s to the 1890s, over 1,000 ships journeyed to South Shetland Islands in order to hunt Fur Seals. During the whaling era, processing plants were established in and around the Antarctic Peninsula and outlying islands such as South Georgia. Whale fragments still litter the coastlines, and the relics of whaling stations and oil storage tanks continue to slowly rust in the unforgiving environment.

Sealing

Sealing was by far the most important economic activity in the Antarctic during the 18th and 19th centuries, dwarfing the exploratory voyages of European and North American sailors and scientists. Lured by the promise of profit, sealers from the United States, the United Kingdom, France, Australia, South Africa, and Chile, descended onto the sub-Antarctic islands and islands close to the Antarctic Peninsula, in the main for Fur Seal pelts.

Gangs of sealers were dispatched to particular beaches in the Antarctic and expected to live in tents during the summer season. Ships would then continue to circle islands and territories in the hunt for further commercial opportunities. The reports by the sealers themselves reveal a brutal, short-term-minded industry motivated by rapacity. The killing of seals was indiscriminate – everything was targeted regardless of age and size. Initially, the sealers killed the seals on the beaches, but subsequently chased them at sea using guns rather than clubs. By the early 1820s, over one million Fur Seal skins were processed, and over 90 vessels were based at South Georgia with as many as 3,000 men working onshore. Later, sealers travelled further south to the South Shetlands to continue their work and virtually eliminated the Fur Seal from this part of the Antarctic. Further afield, sealers were reported to be operating in a range of sub-Antarctic islands, including Prince Edward, Macquarie, and Crozet.

Elephant Seals were hunted, in contrast to the Fur Seal, for their oil, which was rendered from their blubber. The oil was used for lighting, lubricant, and for leather preparation. Islands such as South Georgia, Macquarie, and Heard were important killing grounds. Both types of seals, fortunately for sealers, were easy to target because they formed discrete colonies along the beaches. The breeding grounds were well established, easily locatable, and, once the bull seals were killed, the rest of the colony was easily exploited. Between 1810 and 1920, hundreds of thousands of Elephant Seals were killed. There was some attempt to regulate the extraction rates as far back as the 1870s, but on South Georgia the industry continued until the 1960s, well after Fur Seals were protected. The whaling station at Grytviken in South Georgia serves as a powerful reminder of this trade.

While hundreds of thousands of seals were killed, especially Fur and Elephant varieties, the impact on the Antarctic ecosystem *per se* is harder to judge. Clearly, the extraction of a major predator had implications for other species including krill, penguins, and fish. Seal stocks did recover after 1910, in large part because of conservation measures and licensing introduced in the British-controlled Falkland Islands Dependencies. Restrictions were introduced in South Georgia, which meant that no more than 9,000 Elephant Seal bulls could be killed in any one year within designated sealing areas. Closed seasons were introduced and sealing colonies protected. Between the 1940s and the early 1960s, 250,000 seals were harvested, producing about 75,000 tons of oil. Studies conducted at the time suggested that this level of extraction was sustainable. After 1964, sealing ceased at South Georgia. Some exploratory sealing was carried out elsewhere, but nowhere near the previous levels of exploitation witnessed in the 19th and first half of the 20th centuries.

Scientists monitoring seal populations in the Antarctic believe that the populations have largely recovered, especially since the entry into force of the 1978 Convention for the Conservation of Antarctic Seals, which introduced protective measures for a variety of seals including the Elephant and Fur. Such has been the recovery of the Fur Seal population around South Georgia that there is now concern about the destruction of tussock grass inhabited by penguins and burrowing birds. Part of the difficult judgement to be made about recovering species populations is understanding what kinds of environments islands such as South Georgia enjoyed prior to the onset of sealing. Understanding ecosystem change in places like South Georgia and the South Shetlands needs to take into account another major commercial activity, whaling.

Whaling

Initially, there were inconclusive exploratory voyages by the German Whaling and Sealing Expedition (1873–4) and the Dundee Whaling Expedition (1892–3) of the Weddell Sea and the waters around islands such as South Georgia. The Norwegian naval captain Carl Anton Larsen – the skipper of the 1901–3 Swedish expedition – first noticed big Rorquals (Baleen Whales) and promptly set up a company to exploit them in 1904. With Argentine sponsors, the Compania Argentina de Pesca SA established the first onshore station at Grytviken in South Georgia. As the station manager, Larsen created a distinct Norwegian community, equipped with its own Lutheran Church, negotiating and managing relations with British administrators and Argentine meteorologists. He lived there with his wife and children and eventually became a British citizen.

From 1904 to 1917, South Georgia witnessed an enormous expansion of whaling activities. New stations were established throughout the island, and Norwegian whalers became a permanent presence on this British-administered territory. In the Antarctic itself, the natural harbour within Deception Island provided another base of operations. By 1912, there were 6 onshore stations, 21 floating factories, and 62 whale catchers processing over 10,000 whales. Catchers and floating factories then travelled around the Antarctic Peninsula region seeking further opportunities in the South Orkneys. Fearing over-exploitation, the Colonial Office began to regulate this nascent industry and impose restrictions, especially on Humpback Whales. Licences imposing controls on land-based and inshore operations were issued, and magistrates were appointed to South Georgia in 1909 and on Deception in 1910 to help tax and regulate the industry.

British attempts to impose their authority over Norwegian and other national whaling companies encouraged the second phase of Antarctic whaling. Resenting those taxes and regulation, Norwegian operators introduced pelagic (or open water) whaling to the Antarctic. In 1912–3, three ships unable to reach their harbour in the South Orkneys initiated a new form of whaling. They began hunting on the high seas and then used the edge of an ice field to process the whale carcasses, thereby avoiding the prying gaze of British tax collectors and administrators. Later, custom-made ships such as the *Lancing* were operating in polar waters with a specially designed slipway and haulage system that allowed whales to be dragged onboard rather than onshore.

During the 1920s, when the *Lancing* was cruising Antarctic waters, the British government established the Discovery Investigations, a programme designed to gather further information about whale stocks in order, it was hoped, to avoid a possible collapse of stock numbers. Pelagic whaling, it was feared, would encourage recklessly high levels of exploitation. Subsequent over-activity led whaling countries to press for an International Convention for the Regulation of Whaling (1931), which established protection for cows with calves and immature whales. This was a timely intervention given that in the Southern Ocean there was evidence of decline, especially of Humpback and Blue Whales. What saved whales from further decimation was the intervention of war and the capture by the German navy of the Norwegian pelagic whaling fleet. Between 1941 and 1945, only one factory ship was operating in the Southern Ocean.

The final phase of Antarctic whaling occurred in the post-war period, which witnessed some evidence of commercial revival but with tighter regulations of the industry. Importantly, the American commander in post-war Japan, Douglas MacArthur, authorized the beginning of large-scale Japanese Antarctic whaling. In 1946, the International Convention on the Regulation of Whaling was signed and the International Whaling Commission (IWC) created. The IWC was designed to impose controls over the industry and introduced a quota system based on the so-called Blue Whale Unit (BWU) – a BWU represented one Blue Whale, two Fin Whales, and/or six Sei Whales. Notwithstanding those endeavours to regulate, whaling in South Georgia resumed, and over the next 20 years 3 onshore stations, 20-odd factory ships, and assorted catchers hauled in over 30,000 whales per year. One difficulty the IWC faced during this period was controlling a remote industry in a huge hunting ground, which was loosely regulated at best. The 1954 film *Hell Below Zero* provided a vivid depiction of offshore whaling in the Southern Ocean.

What was to change the whaling industry was not tighter regulation but commercial alternatives coupled with changing public opinion in Europe and North America in the main. Tropical vegetable oil plantations began to replace whale oil in the post-war period, especially for European consumers. Norwegian companies, anticipating further decline in whale oil, withdrew from South Georgia in 1964 and left the industry to a collection of Japanese and Soviet enterprises. At the end of the 1960s, catches dropped to about 12,000 whales, and the onshore stations in South Georgia were abandoned. This decline, coupled with mounting anti-whaling sentiment, had geopolitical implications for Britain. With the decline of the Norwegian whaling industry,

Britain decided that a small party of Royal Marines would need to be permanently located at South Georgia. The strategic rationale was to deter Argentina from invading and occupying the island. In April 1982, an Argentine scrap metal merchant and accompanying party triggered naval operations, which led to the invasion and occupation of the Falkland Islands on 2 April 1982. British and Argentine forces confronted one another on South Georgia, and British Antarctic Survey (BAS) scientists (who were also living and working there) were caught up in the furore. After the Argentines were defeated, BAS established a new base on the island and the UK military presence was scaled back.

While whaling disappeared from South Georgia, the IWC – spurred on by anxieties regarding whale stocks – recommended moratoria and restrictions, culminating in the 1985–6 proposal for a complete prohibition on Southern Ocean whaling. Japan and the Soviet Union objected to this proposal and continued to catch Minke Whales. Later in the same decade, Japan claimed scientific research as the justification for its whaling. While the numbers involved are comparatively small, given past levels of exploitation, the politics of whaling is fiercely contested. There is some evidence of whale recovery, especially involving Humpbacks in and around the Antarctic Peninsula. But as numbers of seals and penguins rise alongside human exploitation of krill and fish, whale numbers may never recover to their 1940s and 1950s levels.

Living resources in international waters and/or territories where sovereignty is disputed provide ideal opportunities for the maximization of exploitation leading to the 'tragedy of commons'. The IWC was intended to introduce a system of regulation and restraint based on scientific knowledge, in a manner pioneered by the Discovery Investigations. Notwithstanding conservation measures and changing public opinion, reductions in whaling were also achieved by the changing political economies of the industry. It is unlikely that commercial whaling will ever return to Antarctica, apart from 'scientific whaling' by Japan.

Fishing

The exploitation of fish in the Southern Ocean took off from
the 1960s onwards. Spurred on by distant water fishing fleets
hailing from the Soviet Union and Eastern Europe, fishing
entered into a new commercial phase after earlier attempts from
the 1930s had failed. Difficult operational conditions and distance
to markets were cited as key inhibitors. In bio-geographical terms,
fish are found in particular places in the Antarctic, including the
krill-rich waters of the Scotia Sea and closer inshore on the
continental shelf areas near to the Antarctic Peninsula, and
sub-Antarctic islands such as South Georgia and South Orkney.
For the next 30 years, Soviet and Eastern European fishing fleets
dominated the extraction of bottom-dwelling fish such as the
Marbled Rockcod. In 1992–3, 2 million tons of fish were caught in
the Atlantic Ocean sector, and 1.7 million tons in the Indian Ocean
sector. More recently, species such as the Mackerel Icefish and the
Patagonian Toothfish have been commercially exploited in the
southern portions of the South Atlantic and Indian Oceans.

Twelve species of fish have been commercially targeted, and fish
that are slow-growing and enjoy low reproduction rates such as the
Patagonian Toothfish are particularly vulnerable to over-exploitation.
Moreover, commercial fishing has negative consequences for the
marine ecosystem. Fishing reduces the total availability of food
supply for other animals including sea birds, seals, and whales, whilst
fishing nets and associated debris pose dangers. Countless examples
of entangled birds and seals are routinely reported, with the most
notorious cases involving albatrosses caught up in longline fishing
around South Georgia and Kerguelen. In the early 1990s, it was
reported that longline fishing activities might have killed around
40,000 albatrosses.

In 1982, the Convention for the Conservation of Antarctic Marine
Living Resources entered into force. The origins of this
development lie in the 1970s and a growing fear that krill and fish

were next to be intensely exploited in the Southern Ocean, following seals and whales. Krill exploitation, for example, was initiated by the Soviet Union in the early 1960s. By 1981/2, over 50,000 tons were captured, with the Soviet Union dominating the krill market. At the height of this commercial over-fishing in the 1970s and 1980s, krill was being widely considered as a potential source of food for the global South. Given its central role in the Southern Oceanic food chain, there was understandable concern for the deleterious consequences facing other living creatures.

The intent of the convention was to introduce conservation measures, based on scientific research, designed to ensure the long-term sustainability of the Antarctic marine ecosystem. Using the Antarctic Convergence as its area of application, and an ecosystem approach, members adopted a series of measures including species prohibitions, minimum net sizes, and, most significantly, total allowable catches (TACs). The TAC sets the maximum level of exploitation and varies depending on species and geographical area (a series of managerial regions are defined, such as South Georgia being sub-region 48.3) around the polar continent. In terms of maintaining credibility, a scientific committee advises the Convention for the Conservation of Antarctic Marine Living Resources (CCAMLR) policy-making commission.

Additionally, under the terms of the so-called bi-focal approach, claimant states such as Britain, France, Australia, and South Africa are able to enact additional measures designed to protect their sovereign rights in and around sub-Antarctic islands. This was an important development because the move to adopt the Antarctic Convergence as the zone of application meant that the waters around the sub-Antarctic islands were embraced by CCAMLR conservation measures. Claimants such as the UK interpret the bi-focal approach as confirming their coastal state jurisdiction over island and polar continental territories, while non-claimants tend to understand this approach as merely referring to islands within the Convention area but north of 60ºS.

One of the principal challenges confronting the management of Southern Ocean fisheries is illegal, unregulated, and unreported fishing (IUU). Illegal fishing refers to fishing by CCAMLR parties which are in breach of CCAMLR conservation measures, or vessels fishing in an exclusive economic zone of a coastal state without permission. Unreported fishing refers to fishing not reported to CCAMLR or another competent body. Unregulated fishing highlights the problem of third parties, not members of CCAMLR, fishing in high seas.

These different forms of fishing came to the fore in the 1990s when the exploitation of Patagonian Toothfish triggered public and scientific scrutiny. This revealed the difficulties facing regulators and conservationists trying to restrict a trade worth millions, and touching upon troubling issues such as regulating fishing in remote areas, weak importation controls, flagged and re-flagged fishing vessels, incomplete catch information, and the problematic role of third parties who are not members of CCAMLR. In 1994–5, it was thought that as much as 115, 000 tons of Toothfish was being harvested rather than the total reported catch of nearly 9,000 tons.

In the last decade, CCAMLR and claimant states such as Australia, Britain, and France have pushed for further measures designed to address IUU fishing, ranging from having observers on board licensed fishing vessels to better catch-documentation schemes. Some of the vessels engaged in IUU fishing are registered to CCAMLR members, and the power to inspect and regulate, let alone detain, is limited and contested. Argentina resents the fact that Britain sells fishing licences to exploit the waters around South Georgia and, further north, the Falkland Islands. Countries such as Australia, claimant of the Heard and MacDonald Islands, have invested more heavily in fisheries protection and been prepared to chase and apprehend vessels suspected of fishing illegally in the waters around its islands. IUU fishing is a problem involving third parties and other CCAMLR members who are reluctant to restrain a lucrative trade in Southern Ocean fisheries – contrast this with the mutual inspection system of scientific stations on the polar continent.

Reducing illegal fishing will involve a combination of procedures such as fisheries protection, trans-shipment inspection regimes in countries such as Namibia, Mauritius, and Madagascar, combined with renewed consumer pressure. The Marine Stewardship Council has certified the South Georgia fishing ground as sustainable, involving a TAC of approximately 3,000 tons per year (some five to ten times less than illegal fishing quantities). A Coalition of Legal Toothfish Operators helps to represent those fishing companies abiding by licensing regulations, effective in the Southern Ocean. There are signs that illegal fishing involving Patagonian Toothfish is abating due to consumer and conservation-related measures. The Australian Antarctic Division declared in 2011 that:

> Through increased controls on harvesting and trade by CCAMLR and significant enforcement efforts by Australia and France, illegal unreported and unregulated (IUU) fishing for toothfish has declined to near-zero levels in waters under national jurisdiction. Some IUU fishing persists elsewhere in the CCAMLR Area and was estimated at about 1300 tonnes in 2010.

Illegal fishing is unlikely to be removed from the Southern Ocean. The potential rewards are still considerable, notwithstanding enforcement efforts of regulatory bodies such as CCAMLR who struggle to reconcile the fact that some of the worst offenders are actually members of the very body intended to promote sustainable living resource extraction.

Mineral resources

Mineral resources were first discovered in the first decade of the last century. Frank Wild, a member of the Shackleton expedition of 1907–9, spotted a coal seam on the Beardmore Glacier. No one at the time considered them remotely exploitable, but the seams (and the fossils within them) did help to confirm the Antarctic's earlier geological history and its physical relationship to southern Africa, India, Australia, and South America. Since that expedition, generations of geologists, geophysicists, marine biologists, and oceanographers played their part in exploring and recording traces of minerals both on the polar continent and offshore. As visitors to the Antarctic Peninsula would swiftly discover, evidence for mineralization is not hard to find. Green-stained cliffs and mountains hint at the presence of copper alongside other traces of iron, nickel, cobalt, lead, gold, and silver. Overall, mineral resource prospects in the Antarctic Peninsula are judged to be modest, and coal seams in the Trans-Antarctic Mountains vary in quality and quantity ranging from bituminous to anthracitic. Elsewhere, occurrences of iron, lead, uranium, and zinc have been recorded in East Antarctica in Dronning Maud, Enderby Land, and alongside the coal-bearing strata of the Prince Charles Mountains. Again, the general view suggests that these areas might be worthy of further examination but they are not considered to be of high economic potential.

Speculation about future resource wealth has instead focused offshore. A 1974 US Geological Survey Report suggested that oil and gas might, one day, be found in commercial quantities, leading to a slew of headlines about Antarctica's potential to be the polar equivalent of the Middle East in hydrocarbon terms. Coinciding as it did with the OPEC 'oil shock', this was hyperbole. At the current time, there has been no commercial drilling, and earlier projects such as the Deep Sea Drilling Project (DSDP) and Ocean Drilling Program were scientific ventures not mainly concerned with prospecting for oil and gas deposits. The DSDP, for example, did encounter traces of natural gas in the Ross Sea in the early 1970s, but its remit was to study and gather materials from the ocean floor around the world. Hydrocarbon exploitation would encounter a continental shelf with average depths of

500 metres, and there are neo-tectonic hazards to boot such as faulting and volcanism. Onshore sedimentary basins that might prove geologically of interest are under thick ice, and thus unlikely to attract any commercial interest, even if mineral exploitation were ever permitted.

The Protocol on Environmental Protection currently bans all forms of mining and mineral exploitation. An earlier attempt to negotiate an agreement specifically regarding mineral resources (the Convention on the Regulation of Antarctic Mineral Resources, CRAMRA) floundered in the 1980s because two claimant states, Australia and France, walked away from the agreement. Sensing hostile public opinion and criticism from Third World states, CRAMRA was never adopted. Although CRAMRA was trying to establish potential rules for future exploitation, it set off a tsunami of criticism. At that moment in the early 1980s, there was no commercial, legal, or political pressure to exploit mineral resources in the Antarctic. It remains, some 20-plus years later, a remote and expensive potential operating environment. Far more productive and accessible areas exist elsewhere, including the Arctic Ocean. Even if there were commercial potential, in the longer term, the cost of extraction would be high as everything would have to be shipped in and out of Antarctica at considerable expense – there is no existing infrastructure, the climate is hostile, there are few natural harbours, it is remote, and generally more extreme than working conditions typically encountered in the Arctic such as iceberg-filled waters. While some aspects of Arctic-related technology would be transferable, the operating and logistical problems confronting miners is of a higher order.

Future resource challenges

The resource potential of the Antarctic, notwithstanding the provisions of the Protocol on Environment Protection, is unsettling precisely because it brings to the fore the unresolved status of claimant and non-claimant alike. Resource-related issues can be used to demonstrate how this sovereignty dilemma plays out in a variety of cultural, political, and legal contexts, often far removed from the Antarctic itself. For example, the implications of sovereign rights being recognized on the seabed off the polar continent is a divisive issue. However careful some claimants have been to ask the UN body, the Commission on the Limits of the Continental Shelf, not to formally consider their Antarctic data, the seven claimants all act as if they believe that they are coastal states in the Antarctic. Most ostentatiously, Argentina made a submission in April 2009 that included a map detailing outer continental shelf limits in the deeply contested Antarctic Peninsula region. Interestingly, as if recognizing the potential for this issue to be troublesome, the parties issued a Ministerial Declaration on the 50th anniversary of the Antarctic Treaty in April 2009 reaffirming that 'the importance they attach to the contribution made by the Treaty, and by Article IV in particular, to ensuring the continuance of international harmony in Antarctica'. To reinforce this apparent display of unity and restraint, the provisions of Article 7 of the Protocol were noted, prohibiting mineral resource exploitation in the Antarctic.

All very laudable, perhaps, but the delimitation of outer continental shelves is problematic. If states such as New Zealand make partial submissions (as in 2006), then they might make full submissions in the future. And if they do so, then they bring to the fore the status of national sovereignty claims in the Antarctic. Moreover, any submission is surely going to provoke well-known non-claimants including China, India, Russia, and the United States to conclude that these submissions represent extensions of claims made in 1959 on the eve of the Antarctic Conference. The temptation then arises for non-claimants to 'walk away' from the treaty and its key provision regarding sovereignty abeyance. The decision to submit partial submissions on the part of claimant states is then a calculated one – to register one's interest without alienating the non-claimant community. For claimants in particular, the preservation of the ATS has been fundamental to their preservation of sovereignty claims, and one would think that continental shelf mineral resources (with all the attendant difficulties of recovery and exploitation) would not be worth any potential damage to the ATS as an international regime.

Whaling is another major worry for the ATS that brings to the fore sovereignty politics. The most visible manifestation of this tension exists between Australia and the non-claimant Japan. The International Whaling Commission (IWC), the major regulatory body with regard to whaling, created in 1986 a moratorium on commercial whaling in the Southern Ocean. In 1994, the IWC sanctioned the creation of the Southern Ocean Whale Sanctuary, and this was widely supported in anti-whaling nations such as Australia. The root cause of the conflict lies in a long-standing enmity between the two countries about a loophole regarding whaling. There is scope for some 'scientific' whaling in the Southern Ocean, and in 2005 Japan initiated a whale research programme (JAPRA II) and issued permits to Japanese whaling companies. Disputing the number of whales that might need to be killed for such research, Australian ire was further increased when it became clear that a great deal of whale meat was being sold in Japanese fish markets. This is also a telling issue because it reveals that science alone cannot determine legitimacy regarding Antarctic activity.

Within Australia, the legal process pertaining to whaling has become ever more prohibitive. In 1980, the Whale Protection Act was introduced, designed to enhance protection for whales within Australian waters. This was reinforced in 1999 with the Environment Protection and Biodiversity Conservation Act, which established an Australian Whale Sanctuary (AWS) encompassing all Australian territories including the Australian Antarctic Territory. Whaling is prohibited as a consequence, and successive Australian governments have expressed disapproval of Japanese whaling, scientific or not. In 2004, the Humane

Society International (HSI), a public interest organization, brought a case to the Australian Federal Court against a Japanese whaling company, Kyodo Senpaku Kaisha Ltd. The HSI argued that this whaling operator was killing whales illegally in the AWS, and in particular in the waters off the Australian Antarctic Territory. The Court issued a judgment in favour of HSI by concluding that, within the provisions of the EPBC Act and UNCLOS, the Japanese company violated Australian law. They issued an injunction in January 2008 demanding that no whales within the AWS be killed, injured, and/or taken. Australia, in effect, became the first claimant state (and state in general) to find that Japanese whaling in the Southern Ocean was illegal. In response, Japan declared that it proposed to ignore the court's ruling and advised companies registered in the country to do the same, on the basis that it does not recognize Australia's capacity to proclaim the AWS in the first place. Japan contends, along with many others, that these waters are in effect high seas.

10. Conflict over Japanese 'scientific whaling' in the Southern Ocean

In June 2010, Australia began proceedings against the Japanese government in the ICJ, arguing that the continued whaling programme is in violation of obligations undertaken by Japan regarding whaling and marine mammal protection. Japan will no doubt argue that 'scientific whaling' is permissible under the terms of the International Convention for the Regulation of Whaling (Article 8), and that there are no agreed coastal states in the Antarctic to enforce national whaling sanctuaries. With the help of non-governmental organizations such as the Sea Shepherd Society, which has a track record of directly confronting Japanese whalers (raising an interesting question about whether this does violate the terms of the Antarctic Treaty pertaining to peaceful purposes), Australia is perhaps hoping to internationally shame Japan rather than secure a definitive legal judgment in its favour.

The final resource issue that might be problematic in the future is perhaps the least well publicized. While public opinion is well versed in the whaling debate, the same cannot be said for biological prospecting. Scientific investigation of fauna and flora is generating commercially valuable information on genetic and biochemical resources. Anti-freeze proteins, krill oil, and food-related products have all been generated from Antarctic-related research activities. It is estimated that something in the order of 200 companies and research organizations including Du Pont, Oxford University, and Unilever are involved in biological prospecting. Over 25 states are represented, including the United States, Japan, China, India, the United Kingdom, and Russia; a mixture, therefore, of claimant and non-claimant states alike. Antarctic krill have produced rich pickings, and Japan is one of the largest operators in the Antarctic, according to the Antarctic Bio-Prospecting Database (<http://www.bioprospector.org>).

The potential for conflict resides in the uneasy relationship between a key article of the Antarctic Treaty (relating to freedom of scientific information exchange) and commercial imperatives.

Biological prospecting is profit-driven, even if the research scientists who conduct it are committed to furthering basic research into biological organisms. If the profit motive prevails, would concerns regarding commercial sensitivity impair the requirement to cooperate and exchange information? Does intellectual property rights law further prohibit free exchange if the Antarctic's genetic resources are subject to further commoditization? All of this brings to the fore again the sovereignty dilemma. Biological prospecting, especially if it was tied to substantial revenue generation, would raise concerns about how access to Antarctica's genetic resources was being regulated or not. Might claimant states ever be tempted to try and impose, however indirectly, further controls on how and who has the authority to biologically prospect in certain parts of the Antarctic? And should there be any attempt to share any monies generated by this activity within the ATCPs or wider international community given that the sovereign status of the Antarctic is unclear?

Protecting Antarctica

Under the terms of the Protocol on Environmental Protection, the Antarctic is designated as a 'natural reserve, devoted to peace and science'. Article 3 stipulates that:

> The protection of the Antarctic environment and dependent and associated ecosystems and the intrinsic value of Antarctica, including its wilderness and aesthetic values and its value as an area for the conduct of scientific research, in particular research essential to understanding the global environment, shall be fundamental considerations in the planning and conduct of all activities in the Antarctic Treaty area.

The Protocol was intended to be comprehensive even if there is no definition of wilderness and wilderness values anywhere in the text, which has led to ambiguity and confusion over what exactly is being protected, and which element of the ATS is best suited to execute environmental protection.

The Protocol's objective is the 'comprehensive protection of the Antarctic environment and dependent and associated ecosystems', and parties are urged to consider a precautionary approach seeking to avoid adverse environmental damage. All activities are subject to environmental impact assessment (EIA) using a three-tiered approach based on likely impact and associated severity. An advisory Committee for Environmental Protection (CEP), established under the Protocol, helps with implementation matters that extend to both terrestrial and marine environments. This has, however, led to some uncertainty because it is not clear whether CCAMLR should take the lead when it comes to establishing, for example, marine protected areas. CCAMLR parties, including those states with substantial fishing interests, were often slow to respond to area closures, but now work with the CEP to implement such marine closure measures.

The environmental protection of the Antarctic is not simply a matter for the Protocol. It is part of a wider web of environmental agreements that stretch and contain the Antarctic. In the realm of fishing, CCAMLR and the Protocol in different ways address the marine environment. But so do others. The Convention for the Conservation of Southern Bluefin Tuna (CCSBT) addresses the management of this particular fish species, regardless of location. Its remit does not cease at the Antarctic Convergence. While fish stocks are to be found in the southern portions of the Indian and Pacific Oceans, it was discovered that Japan in 2005 was exploiting this species in the CCAMLR zone of application. This fishing was not authorized by either CCSBT or CCAMLR. There was no coordination between the parties and, to this day, there remains no resolution about how to manage the respective terms and conditions.

This problem of overlap and conflicting jurisdictions is not unique to fish in the Antarctic. Variations do exist in the coordination and cooperation between the conventions and their parties. A good example is the Agreement on the Conservation of Albatrosses and Petrels (ACAP), which entered into force in 2001 and was designed to encourage these species' conservation, especially given fears over sea bird mortality due to fishing in the Southern Ocean. Unlike in the case of the Bluefin Tuna, CCAMLR and ACAP parties have worked closely with one another to share information on sea bird population in the Southern Ocean. The key difference between the Albatross and the Bluefin Tuna, however, is the value of the resource in question. It appears to be a lot easier to collaborate when the species concerned is not commercially exploitable.

Other areas of potential overlap and conflict include the Convention on Biological Diversity (CBD) and the United Nations Convention on the Law of the Sea (UNCLOS). The CBD, for instance, sits uneasily with the ATS and the development of biological prospecting. While the ATS remains unable to trumpet a comprehensive regulatory approach, the CBD parties have periodically reflected on the growing interest in Antarctic-based biological prospecting. In the absence of any agreement within the ATS, the consultative parties have had to draw upon rules relating to science management and the strictures imposed by the Protocol itself, especially Article 3. UNCLOS, as we noted with reference to extended continental shelf delimitation, raises not only issues pertaining to exploitation but also conservation on the marine seabed. The non-recognition of continental claims, alongside the provisions of Article IV of the Antarctic Treaty, means that claimant and non-claimant states alike keenly scrutinize any issue pertaining to either exploitation or protection/conservation.

Developed in the aftermath of the ill-fated CRAMRA negotiations, the Protocol's emergence came at a point in time when it was increasingly recognized that present (and future) resource-related challenges are ending Antarctica's isolation from the wider world. The paradox facing those seeking to protect the Antarctic, including its wilderness qualities, is rooted in the fact that we have an enormous area, with little obvious evidence of human presence, being increasingly drawn into networks of human activity including but not restricted to resource exploitation and conservation. Over the decades, sealing, whaling, fishing, mineral exploitation, and biological prospecting present challenges not only to the contested politics of Antarctic sovereignty but also to attempts to manage sustainably. As past episodes of sealing and whaling demonstrate, there is always a capacity for the commons, in this case the Antarctic, to be a tragic case.

Summary

The Antarctic is increasingly facing environmental and resource-related challenges. While we consider the challenges posed by climate change, ozone depletion, and pollution elsewhere, we should note the cumulative impact of resource exploitation in particular. As scholars have warned for decades, in the absence of rules and regulations, there is always a danger that common resource spaces such as the Antarctic and the high seas will be exploited in an unsustainable manner. Seals and whales bore the brunt of that impulse in the 19th and 20th centuries, and illegal, unregulated, and unreported fishing causes contemporary alarm in the Southern Ocean. Balancing initiatives to enhance environmental protection with ongoing and future-orientated resource interests is one of the key challenges facing those managing the Antarctic.

The rejection of CRAMRA in the late 1980s did not mean that mineral resource interests in the Antarctic disappeared. The Protocol bans all forms of mineral exploitation, and does so as long as all parties (including third parties) respect those provisions. While no one expects mining to commence any time soon, the interest shown by coastal states with regard to the extended continental shelf suggests that resource exploitation remains a topic of interest, however remote it might be in the future. Whether promoting fishing interests or seeking to circumvent whaling, claimant states such as Argentina, Australia, New Zealand, and the United Kingdom all retain a keen interest in the resource potential of their Antarctic sectors.

The environmental protection of the Antarctic, in the end, depends on a consensual approach. The negotiations over a minerals convention demonstrated the capacity of resource-related matters to fragment consensus among the parties. While arguably less dramatic, the articulation and introduction of conservation measures can also expose schisms within the consultative parties. This can be the case regardless of whether addressing fishing, specially protected areas, heritage conservation, and/or the likely impact of Antarctic science, such as the establishment of a research station in a particular part of the polar continent. Claimant states tend to be wary of global environmental instruments such as the CBD, not least because the Antarctic Treaty and its associated legal instruments are assumed to be *primus inter pares*. It remains to be seen whether the environmental protection and resource management of the Antarctic will be developed increasingly via global environmental instruments and practice. For many Antarctic parties, including claimant states, this would be a truly alarming prospect, especially if it was thought that sovereign rights might be diluted.

Final thoughts

The Antarctic, as far as it has been imagined and experienced by humans, has stimulated and enriched fantasies, bodies of knowledge, and myths. Antarctica has inspired hope and fear. The world's only continent without an indigenous human population continues to attract geographical representations pertaining to its status as a global wilderness and/or common heritage of humankind. As global common, Antarctica inspires a limited amount of scholarly commentary about the role of the common good, as opposed to the supposed self-interest of states and others, including corporations, minded to exploit and develop the 'ends of the earth'. In the 1980s, rather more than in the 2010s, there was interest in various hydrocarbon futures for the Antarctic, but this has largely been subsumed by the ban on mineral exploitation imposed by the Protocol on Environmental Protection. If anything, attention has turned once again to the Arctic as a more immediate source of additional oil, gas, and other resources including iron ore and zinc.

The contemporary Antarctic remains locked within two fundamental forces. On the one hand, 'the Antarctic Problem', a term first used in the late 1940s, remains. Claimant states believe that they enjoy territorial sovereignty over parts of the Antarctic, and Article IV allowed them to continue to believe that this was the case. Politically, the price of being a claimant remains modest, as they do not attract opprobrium from other members and continue to cement their sovereign pretensions within domestic cultures. On the other hand, the Antarctic is being commercially exploited and developed in ways that were not anticipated some 60 years ago. Empowered by neo-liberal ideology and practice, the commercialization of the Antarctic continues apace. Fishing, tourism, and biological prospecting, and possibly non-living resource extraction in the future, will provoke fresh concerns over the ownership of the polar continent and its continental shelves.

The Antarctic faces multiple futures on an increasingly hot and overcrowded planet – and future resource needs will have an important role to play.

Further reading

There is a series of specialist academic journals addressing the Antarctic, including *Antarctic Science*; *Arctic, Antarctic and Alpine Research*; *Polar Journal*; *Polar Record*; and *Polar Research*. Two helpful encyclopedias are Bernard Stonehouse's *Encyclopedia of Antarctica and the Southern Oceans* (Chicester: John Wiley, 2002), and Beau Riffenburgh's *Encyclopedia of the Antarctic* (London: Routledge, 2007). There is, of course, no shortage of literature aimed at children, especially in the UK, where the Antarctic is studied at school as part of modules on cold environments. Interested readers should simply consult well-known commercial websites (e.g. Amazon) for further details.

Chapter 1 Defining the Antarctic

A popular guide, especially with Antarctic tourists, is Jeff Rubin's *Antarctica* (London: Lonely Planet, 2008). Other introductory texts for the general reader include David McGonigal's *Antarctica: Secrets of a Southern Continent* (London: Frances Lincoln, 2009), and David McGongial and Lynn Woodworth's *Antarctica: The Blue Continent* (London: Frances Lincoln, 2005). For an example of a well-regarded travel memoir, see Sara Wheeler's *Terra Incogntia: Travels in Antarctica* (London: Vintage, 2010). For younger readers, see Lucy Bowman's *Antarctica* (London: Usborne, 2007). For a comparative analysis of the Arctic and Antarctic, see Henry Pollack, *A World without Ice* (New York: Avery, 2010), and David Sugden's *Arctic and Antarctic: A Modern Geographical Synthesis* (Oxford: Blackwell, 1982). For a theoretically sophisticated analysis of the cultural politics associated with the Antarctic, see Elena Glasberg's *Antarctica as Cultural Critique* (Basingstoke: Palgrave, 2012).

Chapter 2 Discovering the Antarctic

Classic accounts of Antarctic exploration in the 'Heroic Age' include Apsley Cherry-Gerrard's *The Worst Journey in the World* (Harmondsworth: Penguin, 2006). Before the Heroic era of exploration, see Thomas Baughman's *Before the Heroes Came* (Lincoln: University of Nebraska Press, 1994). There is a massive literature on Scott and Amundsen, including Max Jones's *Last Great Quest* (Oxford: Oxford University Press, 2004), and Edward Larson's *An Empire on Ice* (New Haven: Yale University Press, 2010). One of the most controversial assessments remains Roland Huntford's *Race for the South Pole* (London: Continuum, 2010). For a basic account on the discovery process, see Bernard Stonehouse's *The Last Continent: Discovering Antarctica* (London: SCP Books, 2000). Paul Simpson-Housley's *Exploration, Perception and Metaphor* (London: Routledge, 1992) provides a literary account of polar exploration. For a well-written account of Shackleton's 'great escape' from the Antarctic, see Caroline Alexander's *The Endurance: Shackleton's Legendary Antarctic Expedition* (New York: Knopf Books, 1998), and for his less well-known Nimrod expedition, see Beau Riffenburgh's *Shackleton's Forgotten Expedition* (New York: Bloomsbury, 2005). The latter also penned *Polar Exploration* (London: André Deutsch, 2009). On the role of women and the Antarctic, see Elizabeth Chipman's *Women on the Ice* (Melbourne: Melbourne University Press, 1986). For an encyclopedic collection on expeditions, see Robert Headland's *Chronological List of Antarctic Expeditions and Related Historical Events* (Cambridge: Cambridge University Press, 1990). On Antarctic tourism, see Thomas Bauer's *Tourism in the Antarctic* (London: Routledge, 2002).

Chapter 3 Claiming and negotiating the Antarctic

For an account of how the Antarctic was claimed and 'carved up' amongst the claimant states, see Peter Beck's *International Politics of Antarctica* (London: Croom Helm, 1986), and a classic earlier account remains William Hunter Christie's *The Antarctic Problem*

(London: George Unwin, 1951). On Britain and its geopolitical relationship to the Antarctic, see Klaus Dodds' *Pink Ice: Britain and the South Atlantic Empire* (London: I. B. Tauris, 2002). On the role of Richard Byrd and US Antarctic endeavour, see Lisle Rose's *Explorer: The Life of Richard E. Byrd* (Kansas City: University of Missouri Press, 2008), and for America's Antarctic interests more generally, Chris Joyner and Ethel Theis's *Eagle over the Ice: US in the Antarctic* (Dover: University Press of New England, 1997). Tom Griffiths provides a well-written part memoir and part historical analysis of the 'scramble for the Antarctic' in *Slicing the Silence: Voyaging to Antarctica* (Sydney: University of New South Wales Press, 2007).

Chapter 4 Governing the Antarctic

For two geopolitical accounts of Antarctica's transformation in the 20th century, see Sanjay Chaturvedi's *The Polar Regions: A Political Geography* (Chichester: John Wiley, 1996), and Klaus Dodds' *Geopolitics in Antarctica: Views from the Southern Oceanic Rim* (Chichester: John Wiley, 1997). For a good overview of the Antarctic Treaty System, see Chris Joyner's *Governing the Frozen Commons* (Columbia: University of South Carolina Press, 1998), and see also Olav Stokke and Davor Vidas's edited book *Governing the Antarctic* (Cambridge: Cambridge University Press, 1997). For a legal perspective, Gillian Triggs's *The Antarctic Treaty Regime: Law, Environment and Resources* (Cambridge: Cambridge University Press, 1987) – this remains a reliable guide of the period between the 1960s and late 1980s. For a more recent assessment of the Antarctic Treaty System, Paul Berkman, Michael Lang, David Walton, and Oran Young's edited collection *Science Diplomacy: Antarctica, Science and the Governance of International Spaces* (Washington, DC: Smithsonian Institute, 2011) contains some pertinent contributions.

Chapter 5 Doing Antarctic science

Peder Roberts's *The European Antarctic* (Basingstoke: Palgrave, 2011) provides an essential imperial and colonial contextualization of Antarctic science. George Fogg's *A History of Antarctic Science* (Cambridge: Cambridge University Press, 2005), and David Walton's edited collection *Antarctic Science* (Cambridge:

Cambridge University Press, 1987), remain indispensable. On Antarctica, ice sheets, and changing climatic cycles, see Fabio Florindo and Martin Seigert's edited collection *Antarctic Climate Evolution* (Amsterdam: Elsevier Science, 2008). Meredith Hooper's is an elegant account of contemporary science and the scientific station: *The Ferocious Summer: Palmer's Penguins and the Warming of Antarctica* (London: Profile Books, 2007).

Chapter 6 Exploiting and protecting the Antarctic

For accessible accounts of resource exploitation and environmental conservation in the Antarctic, see *inter alia* Richard Laws's *Antarctica: The Final Frontier* (London: Jordan Box Tree, 1989), and Grahame Cook's edited book *The Future of Antarctica* (Manchester: Manchester University Press, 1990). On mining and 1980s debates pertaining to the Antarctic, see Maarten de Wit's *Minerals and Mining in Antarctica* (Oxford: Oxford University Press, 1986). For a skilful analysis of anti-whaling rhetoric, see Charlotte Epstein's *Power of Words in International Relations: Birth of an Anti-Whaling Discourse* (Boston: MIT Press, 2008). On environmental protection and the Protocol on Environmental Protection, see Davor Vidas's edited collection *Implementing the Environmental Protection Regime for the Antarctic* (Dordrecht: Kluwer Academic Publishers, 2000). For a gloomy prediction for the future of the polar regions, see Peter Ward's *The Flooded Earth: Our Future in a World without Ice Caps* (New York: Basic Books, 2010). A fine novel premised on resource exploitation is Kim Stanley Robinson's *Antarctica* (New York: Bantam Books, 1999).

Index

Index

Expand your collection of
VERY SHORT INTRODUCTIONS